UNIVERSITY OF
GLOUCESTERSHIRE
at Cheltenham and Gloucester

New Creative Accounting

Ian Griffiths

NEW CREATIVE ACCOUNTING

How to make your profits what you want them to be

First published 1995 by
MACMILLAN PRESS LTD
Houndmills, Basingstoke, Hampshire RG21 6XS
and London
Companies and representatives
throughout the world

ISBN 0–333–62865–9

A catalogue record for this book is available
from the British Library.

10   9   8   7   6   5   4   3   2
04   03   02   01   00   99   98   97   96

Printed and bound in Great Britain by
Antony Rowe Ltd, Chippenham, Wiltshire

Contents

Introduction

Every company in the country is fiddling its profits. Every set of accounts is based on books which have been gently cooked or completely roasted.

That was the assertion made in the original version of *Creative Accounting* when it was first published in 1986. Much may have changed in the intervening years but the basic premise still holds true. While many of the more flagrant abuses of the flexible accounting regime with which this country was once blessed have been outlawed those who are charged with the responsibility of preparing a set of accounts still have an extensive range of techniques available to them which can be used to massage the figures which are presented to the watching world.

This is not a criticism of the Accounting Standards Board which was set up in 1990 to bring some order to the chaos which then passed for a regulatory framework. Indeed under Sir David Tweedie's leadership the ASB has made tremendous progress in restoring the credibility and integrity of accounting standards.

Rather, it reflects the imprecise nature of a financial reporting process requiring every company to present accounts each year which reflect a true and fair view of how the business has fared. This never was and never can be an exact science. Instead it is a subtle combination of objective fact and subjective assumption. Except in the simplest cash-based businesses it is impossible, even with the best will in the world, to produce accounts which are anything other than an approximation which have their basis in the transactions and events of the year under review.

How close that approximation is to the original starting-point will depend on a number of factors. Creative accounting represents the means by which that deviation will be achieved.

The big problem facing investors is that there is nothing illegal in companies using to their best advantage accounting rules which are drafted to allow accounts preparers a high degree of flexibility. That flexibility is given not because of any laxity on the part of the standard setters but simply to give the regulatory framework a fighting chance of having a degree of relevance for those who must be guided by it.

The biggest difficulty is that companies are required to report annually. As a period of accountability there is a lot to be said for the twelve-month cycle. Unfortunately it has no relevance at all to the natural business cycle of any company you care to mention. A baked-bean manufacturer would have a cycle which was measured in weeks. A construction company would, however, have a cycle measured in years. Yet both are obliged to report their results on an annual basis and to report them using the same accounting standards.

It is this mismatch between the reporting and business cycles together with the need for a common set of standards to apply to all industries which provides the need and the justification for flexibility. It is flexibility which feeds creative accounting. And it is creative accounting which in the wrong hands can undermine the credibility of a set of accounts.

In this accounting chain the logical conclusion to be drawn is that the greater the degree of flexibility in accounting standards the higher the risk that the quality of reported figures will be distorted. This was indeed the case in the mid to late eighties where a combination of a weak accounting standards setting regime and an orgy of self-indulgent corporate activity conspired to erode significantly the integrity of financial reporting.

It was against this backdrop that Sir Ron Dearing's committee was established by the accountancy profession to make recommendations on the standard setting process. His conclusions, presented in September 1988, were to provide the basis for the creation of the new regime of which the Accounting Standards Board represents the cornerstone.

The timing of his report was helpful for the cause of reform, coming as it did towards the end of the eighties take-over boom and just before the onset of recession. It was in the field of acquisition and merger accounting that some of the most outrageous abuses had been developed. Encouraged perhaps by weak and feeble standard setting a variety of techniques was developed which allowed some acquisitive companies to paint a more positive picture of their position than reality could ever justify.

There were enough warnings about the dangers of an overenthusiastic use of creative accounting. Indeed every contested take-over seemed to involve at some point a vitriolic attack on the quality of the opposition's accounting policies. Unfortunately no one was prepared to pay too much attention and it was only when some of the acquisition-driven conglomerates began to unravel in the face of a less benevolent trading climate that concern began to mount. A series of high profile corporate collapses provided the most compelling argument for reform of the standard setting process. Accounting policies which were accepted without question while share prices were on the way up were discredited as companies came tumbling down.

That reform was spearheaded by the ASB which assumed responsibility for standard setting in its own right in August 1990. There was much to differentiate it from the old Accounting Standards Committee which it replaced and therefore every reason to hope that it would have a greater degree of success in constructing a framework which was more in keeping with the demands of the nineties.

Perhaps most importantly the ASB is independent. Its predecessor had merely been acting on behalf of the Consultative Committee of Accountancy Bodies, the umbrella organization for the profession. The whole process was cumbersome and lacked any real degree of authority and self-confidence. The ASC had no full-time chairman and lacked the focus which was desperately needed. It relied extensively on the goodwill and support of practitioners who were becoming increasingly frustrated by the steadily eroding reputation of the ASC.

Neither could the ASC respond quickly to the issues of the day. At one point a new standard was published even though a loophole to render it worse than useless had already been devised. It was considered in those days that any standard, no matter how defective, was better than no standards at all.

Under the new regime that has changed. The ASB does not operate in isolation and is supported by a number of other bodies. It is overseen by the Financial Reporting Council which provides a broadly based umbrella committed to the promotion of good financial reporting.

More important, however, are two other bodies which have given the new regime a turn of pace and the teeth which had not previously existed. The pace is provided by the Urgent Issues Task Force which was set up by the ASB in 1991 to give it the ability to respond much more swiftly to emerging questions which demand quick action.

The pace of development of new accounting techniques quickened considerably during the eighties to an extent where they quite easily outstripped the cumbersome standard setting process. They were not just outwitting new standards; they were touching the parts which had not yet been considered let alone actually reached. That was not a reflection of the cunning creative accountant poring carefully over the small print of standards and devising ingenious ways to bend the rules. Many of the techniques were developed to reflect rapidly changing business and financing practices.

A slow, inefficient and uncertain regime was easily overwhelmed. However, the problem of dealing with refinements to and new interpretations of the rules and regulations did not disappear with the arrival of the ASB. If the flow of contentious questions slackened it was a function of economic slowdown rather than a sudden upsurge in accounting correctness. The

UITF was established specifically to bring clarity by offering authoritative rulings on the practices in question. This mechanism has allowed the ASB to clamp down on specific abuses without having to go through the process of redrafting a standard entirely.

If the UITF gave the new watchdog more spritely legs then its teeth were provided by the Financial Reporting Review Panel. This was set up to deal with any departures from the reporting obligations of the Companies Act. More importantly it has the power to force a company to redraft its financial statements if these are deemed not to show the requisite true and fair view. This represents teeth that are sharp. It is not so much the cost of redrafting accounts which represents the penalty but rather the public humiliation.

An independent and more professionally based ASB with the ability to respond to emerging issues and supported by not just the enforcement power of the FRRP but also legislation which was amended in 1989 to require companies for the first time to state whether their accounts had been prepared in accordance with the applicable accounting standards represents an altogether more effective regime than the one it replaced.

Yet despite these improvements creative accounting still flourishes. As we will find in later chapters many of the most basic areas of the profit and loss account and balance sheet can still be manipulated. The ASB has had its greatest success in outlawing the most flagrant abuses but without changing the entire basis of accounts preparation it will struggle, on its own, to erase creative accounting entirely.

The biggest problem it faces is the unwitting conspiracy between the City and industry which ensures that the black and white which so many appear to demand will be condemned always to a murky grey. While much is made of the tension between companies and their investors there is a remarkable overlap in their interests. Both would like to see a steady increase in a business's earnings growth profile. In reality it is rarely achievable. However, that does nothing to diminish the zealous pursuit of this elusive Holy Grail.

It is when there is a demand to use accounting to shift the reported figures ever so slightly away from reality that the potential for problems begins. It is easy to see where that demand comes from. If investors were asked to choose between a company which over a five-year period showed pre-tax profits of £1 million, £2 million, £3 million, £6 million and £8 million and one which showed a profit of £1 million, a loss of £2 million, a profit of £4 million, a profit of £9 million and a profit of £8 million they would always choose the former. Shareholders much prefer a company showing steady growth. Yet over the period the actual net pre-tax profits of both companies is exactly the same at £20 million. The first company has merely used creative accounting to iron out the natural fluctuations of the business cycle.

There is nothing fundamentally wrong with that, many would argue. Indeed it is hard to find a reason why share-holders should be subjected to violent fluctuations when the underlying trend line is upwards. The question which arises, however, is where do you draw the line? That is a matter for debate. Where there is debate there is uncertainty. Where there is uncertainty a judgement needs to be made. When judgements need to be made the creative accountant is operating in the most fertile ground available.

There is nothing wrong with smoothing out confusing distortions. But it is a thin line between that and using creative accounting to introduce distorting confusion into the financial statements. The problem both for companies and investors is that the flexibility which is so essential to make sense of a company's trading performance can quite easily make the reported numbers a nonsense. When creative accounting is used to try to reverse the business trend rather than give it more clarity then there is real danger for all involved in the process. Creative accounting can do many things but it cannot save a company which is in difficulties because of fundamental trading problems.

It was when companies began to creak and crumble that investors really began to sit up and take notice. The sudden realization that stated earnings were not necessarily a reliable guide to the underlying strength of a business provided the greatest spur for a renewed interest from the investment community in the quality of financial reporting. That interest has certainly helped the ASB's cause. However, it has not always been translated into the kind of positive involvement in the process that some would have liked. Although there has been a concerted attempt by the ASB to get investors more actively involved in the overall process there has been surprisingly little active support. Everybody agrees that they would like to see an improvement in reporting quality but there are fewer who have ideas on how this might be achieved.

It has been said that it is often easier to describe what you don't want than what you do want, and so it is with accounting standards. There was disquiet with the old system but as far as a new regime is concerned investors really want the impossible. What they would like is to have perfect accounting information on which they can base their investment judgements. But as we already know accounting is an imperfect science.

There is a further confusion because of the fixation with the single number approach to assessing corporate performance. There is a peculiar thirst for a single snapshot figure which allows instant assessment of how a company is doing. Traditionally that role has been filled by the earnings per share figure. What Sir David Tweedie at the ASB has been doing is to try to wean people away from one number and persuade them to look at a whole range of indicators.

It is an entirely sensible approach but it does rely upon the users to take much more interest in a set of accounts than they have done traditionally. Part of the problem here is that there is residual disenchantment with financial reporting. The task for the ASB is therefore not just to provide clearer and more decisive rules but also to restore the credibility of accounts in their entirety.

It is all very well obliging companies to improve the level of disclosure in a set of accounts but if no one is ever going to bother to read the document then it is all to no avail.

A further question therefore arises of the relevance of accounts themselves to the investment decision process. More City attention still appears to be focused on a company's preliminary announcement of its results. In many cases these are quite detailed documents, but they can never have the scope or authority of the full set of accounts.

Institutional investors and City analysts also have a range of other means at their disposal which they can use to supplement the raw details of a company's financial performance. Most companies are today much more conscious of the need to have good relationships with the City and are prepared to make themselves available to answer questions about the results and to talk about long-term strategy at private meetings. Some would argue that these are much more valuable as decision-making tools than the accounts themselves.

It is not however just the City's lack of detailed interest in the accounting process which provides a stumbling block to a rapid improvement in the quality of financial reporting. Companies themselves are also in danger of inhibiting the rate at which progress can be made.

For while they have been generally quite supportive of the approach which the ASB has taken the fact remains that it has not yet strayed into too many areas of great controversy. The vast majority of companies never bent the rules too far. If you have never benefited from using some of the more outrageous creative accounting techniques you do not miss them when they are gone.

Some companies which relied on sleight of hand have simply gone under. Others have been chastened by their creativity and have been forced to unravel the schemes and policies which once flattered them so generously. Most businesses have found, however, that the recessionary years have forced them to concentrate on some quite basic issues. Few have been in expansionary mode and questions of the longer-term implications of a new reporting regime have tended to be pushed further down the main board agenda.

But with the economic outlook improving and the changes

that the ASB are making nudging closer to more controversial areas there are just the first signs that the corporate sector is beginning to look more closely at those implications. It does not always like what it sees. We are a long way from open revolt but the generally supportive stance of accounts preparers will not always be given in future.

The difficulty for the ASB is that companies believe that they are being subjected to increasing regulation. This can come in any shape or form but it almost inevitably imposes an additional burden. There is a genuinely held fear that they are reaching information overload. There is a danger that the ASB's moves to improve the overall quality will be misinterpreted.

The ASB's reforms also coincide with the introduction of the Cadbury Committee's proposals on corporate governance. The Committee, ironically, had its foundation in the level of dissatisfaction with financial reporting. Its terms of reference demanded that it consider a range of issues in relation to financial reporting and accountability. The first of these was 'The responsibilities of executive and non-executive directors for reviewing and reporting on performance to shareholders and other financially interested parties; and the frequency clarity and form in which information should be provided'.

On the basis of that wording it could be assumed that there would be considerable overlap between the work of the ASB and the work of Cadbury. However, because of the way in which the Cadbury Committee developed its thinking its recommendations became much more concerned with board structure than accounting policies.

The two initiatives are not therefore seen as a response to the same problem; they are viewed as different animals. Cadbury extends regulation rather than supplements the work of the ASB. Against this backdrop it is perhaps not surprising that companies begin to feel under a little bit of pressure.

But there is yet another dynamic at work which colours to a certain extent the attitude of companies to financial reporting. This relates specifically to their communications with the press and the City. Stock Exchange guidelines, designed to clamp down on the leaking of price-sensitive information, have served only to restrict the way in which companies deal with the outside world.

In crude terms, the old system allowed companies to marshal the array of analysts' forecasts of their profits' performance into a tolerable range of acceptability. This was done through an informal system of nods and winks which ensured that those analysts who were out of line with the reality could be guided towards more appropriate territory.

It was a system which worked to everyone's advantage. Whether it was healthy is another matter entirely. However, it meant that when results were finally announced there were never too many great shocks and surprises. This avoided embarrassment on the part of the forecasters and would also protect a company's share price from the kind of excessive volatility which always follows the unexpected.

Under the Stock Exchange's new guidelines this kind of gentle shepherding has been effectively outlawed. Any price-sensitive information must be put into the public domain on a more formal and even-handed basis. The ability to correct misinformed forecasts is therefore restricted to set-piece events. The potential for surprises is therefore greatly increased.

Many companies have devised different approaches designed to give as much assistance as they can but there is still considerable room for error. If a business finds itself in the unfortunate situation where the market's expectations are much greater than the reality can deliver it has two choices: it can put out what would effectively be deemed to be a profits warning with all the grief that this entails; or it can turn to the finance director and see what dodges and wheezes there are which might massage the profits profile towards the City's forecasts.

The corporate sector is faced therefore with a number of pressures which make it more difficult to embrace whole-heartedly the ASB's improved disclosure ethos. There is a natural resistance to being overburdened by reporting and regulatory requirements. There is a greater awareness of accountability and governance and there is a critical City audience which it has less ability to influence.

There is a final piece to today's creative accounting jigsaw – the auditor. Once the butt of cheap jokes he is now the butt of expensive lawsuits. A by-product of the corporate collapse is the search for the guilty party. Unfortunately in these situations there can be no such thing as joint and several liability. Someone is to blame, therefore someone has to pay. It is all very well to point the finger at the company but the very nature of the corporate collapse means there is no chance of extracting financial retribution. It is therefore the auditor who is shuffled uncomfortably into the firing line.

The reason is understandable. How is it, people ask, that a company which in a set of audited accounts is showing a healthy performance can in a matter of months be bankrupt? It is a good question for which there is no satisfactory answer. As auditors are deemed to have deep pockets and comfortable insurance they are natural targets for aggrieved investors.

The problem here is that no one really understands the auditor's role. It is known as the 'expectation gap' which represents the difference between the outside world's view of what the auditor is supposed to do and what a firm is legally and contractually obliged to undertake. If this gap had a geographical equivalent it would be the Grand Canyon, so great is the divergence.

The auditor may have the law on his side but the profession has discovered that this is not a defence guaranteed to secure sympathy in any great degree. There has been something of an attempt by the auditing profession not just to explain itself more clearly but also to move its work more closely towards what is expected of it. Even so firms still find themselves under considerable pressure. A firm's opinion that a set of accounts shows a true and fair view is still nowhere near as reliable as some users believe. That will always expose an auditor to probing and difficult questions when things go wrong. At the same time a firm which is theoretically acting on behalf of shareholders to whom it reports is actually paid by the company and must deal on a daily basis with its executives.

Few directors are crude enough to suggest that a failure by an auditor to endorse a particular accounting policy will jeopardize their position. However, it is a tough old world and companies are always obliged to keep their costs under review. Who is to tell whether a competitive tender for the audit might not produce great savings?

None of this is helpful for the ASB. If neither preparers nor users have the same degree of commitment to its goals and objectives then the danger of ebbing closer towards compromise is increased significantly. And if auditors themselves are not brimming with self-confidence their chance to act as an effective arbiter of good accounting tastes, particularly in an area which is dominated by opinion rather than fact, is much reduced.

It is against this backdrop that the development of the standards setting process and therefore the motivation for creative accounting must be seen. For while the climate has changed superficially many of the basic design faults are still in place.

As the following chapters will demonstrate there is still tremendous scope for manipulation.

1. Presentation

It is not just the figures themselves which can be adjusted to suit a company's particular requirements. For the creative accountant the way the numbers are packaged can also have an important influence. Deciding precisely where in the accounts a particular transaction should be reflected is something of an art form.

This has become increasingly important for the profit and loss account where a combination of the Accounting Standard Board's assault on extraordinary items and the introduction of a new format has highlighted the attractions of positive presentation.

The ASB's initiative, which resulted in the publication of Financial Reporting Standard 3, was driven not just by disenchantment with the abuse of extraordinary items but also by a desire to provide a more rounded picture of a company's profitability. The intention behind the standard is to provide users with all the important information they need to draw more informed conclusions about corporate performance.

The ASB argued when FRS3 was published that it would be no longer credible for those analysing financial statements to alight on some aggregate number presented in the accounts and, without due consideration of its components, deem that to be the sole indicator of a company's performance. This is entirely in keeping with Sir David Tweedie's intention to draw people away from the earnings per share figure around which they have fluttered like moths to a candle for such a long time.

His aim was to move the emphasis away from simple headline numbers to a presentation of the components of profits, arguing that this makes possible more mature analysis of performance than could be possible by merely relying upon the bottom line. He is insistent that a company's performance cannot be encapsulated in a single number.

To support this argument the ASB introduced a new primary statement called the Statement of Total Recognized Gains and Losses. It is designed to highlight gains and losses taken to reserves which might otherwise have escaped notice. FRS3 also introduced two further amplifications to help improve understanding in the shape of a note of historical cost profits and losses and a reconciliation of movements in shareholders' funds.

This is entirely in keeping with the simultaneous attack on extraordinary items which had become one of the most common distortions of a set of company results. In a reporting regime which encouraged users to focus purely on the earnings per share figure the extraordinary item started off as a legitimate mechanism to strip out from the annual profits figure those elements which were quite literally outside the normal course of business. The argument in their favour was entirely logical. If these unusual items were included in the earnings per share figure then investors would be given a misleading impression of performance for the year. Instead, they were disclosed below the line and their effect was not incorporated in earnings for the year.

The definition of an extraordinary item was inherently loose. However, size of itself was not deemed to be the justification for classification in this category. Just because a particular transaction was big did not make it extraordinary. To cater for those items which were part of the normal business but which were unusually large the standards setters created the exceptional category. These items were included as part of earnings for the year and were included above the line but disclosed separately.

There was a distinct incentive then for companies to keep costs below the line and income above. Earnings could be flattered either by treating negative items as extraordinary or positive items as exceptional.

It was a temptation that was difficult to resist. Already loose definitions were stretched even further. The 'let's try it out on the chairman approach' seemed to be the most favoured technique for deciding whether something was extraordinary or exceptional. When told about a big loss on a particular transaction the chairman would respond 'How extraordinary'. News of a substantial profit on an asset disposal would be met with 'Quite exceptional'.

An oversimplification perhaps but it encapsulates quite neatly the sordid and sorry state of affairs which existed in this particular part of the profit and loss account.

The biggest problem was the understatement of costs and losses in the profit and loss account. For while it may be handy occasionally for a company to increase profits through the use of exceptional items it is unhelpful to provide an artificial boost by including profits from transactions which are genuinely extraordinary All that does is create a level of profitability which would be more difficult to match in the following year.

It is an entirely different matter as far as the negatives are concerned. The last thing that companies need is for profits to be depressed by a lumpy exceptional item. Much better to exclude this from the equation altogether. However, this did not always just have implications for the year under review. In some cases companies were incurring significant costs relating to the rationalization and restructuring of businesses which were treated as extraordinary.

The nature of these programmes meant that they would be quite often carried out over a number of accounting periods. However, by taking the costs up front and below the line a company was able to ringfence its profit and loss account and earnings per share from the otherwise negative implications. It was not just in year 1 then that the earnings per share figure was protected. Subsequent years were also protected. For while the actual cash to pay for the rationalization was being paid out in later years the charge was made not against profits for the year but against the provisions which had been set up at the outset and treated as extraordinary.

As we know from the chapter on the profit and loss account the creation of provisions is a very effective way of protecting reported profits.

Since the ASB's inception it has steadily gnawed away at the most obvious abuse of extraordinary items culminating in FRS3 which virtually abolishes them altogether.

By removing the clear incentive for companies to treat some costs as extraordinary by insisting that almost everything be included in the body of the profit and loss account and disclosed as exceptional where necessary the ASB had hoped to remove one of the major abuses of UK accounting. However, for this to succeed entirely requires users to agree with the ASB's assertion that it is no longer appropriate to assess a company by reference to one single figure.

Unfortunately that argument is still to be won. There is still a fondness for the earnings per share figure which is after all a crucial component of the price earnings ratio which remains one of the most durable of investment analysis tools. While there is still an e in the p/e ratio there is an absolute requirement for some earnings per share figure of sorts to be constructed.

The ASB says that earnings per share should be calculated on the profit attributable to equity shareholders of the reporting entity after accounting for minority interests, extraordinary items, preference dividends and other appropriations in respect of preference shares.

Unfortunately that is a figure which will reflect all those items which companies previously removed from the equation by treating them as extraordinary. The natural corollary of this crackdown on extraordinary items is volatility in the earnings per share figure. This is regarded as unhelpful both by companies and by many of their shareholders.

However, as always, there is a solution at hand. It comes this time in the shape of the ASB's permission for a company to present alongside the official ASB approved figure its own earnings per share figure which would be calculated on a different basis altogether.

Widespread use of this option was anticipated right from the outset and the alarm bells were set ringing by the fact that FRS3 was the first standard to contain a dissenting view. It came from Robert Bradfield of stockbrokers Cazenove who is the only representative of accounts users on the ASB.

The basic thrust of his concern was that in the process of providing more information by way of notes to the accounts much less relevant information will be available on the face of the profit and loss account. In particular he was concerned that the new format downgrades the prominence given to the key components of taxation and minority interests.

The abandonment of the extraordinary item also contributed to Bradfield's concern. Not that he was seeking its retention. Far from it. Rather he believed that the abolition of extraordinary items makes it harder to assess the underlying financial implications in the crucial area of business disposals. Traditionally these would have been regarded in the purest of terms as extraordinary items. As such they would be clearly segregated from the earnings per share calculation.

Under FRS3, results attributed to disposals would be disclosed as a separate component in the profit and loss account. However, beyond that they are in theory combined with results relating to underlying trading.

Clearly trading profit is of a much higher quality and very different from profits on disposals. However, under FRS3 the two aspects of profits for the year are combined at the pre-tax level, the after-tax and minorities level and for earnings per share.

Bradfield's fear was that these important indicators are distorted on the face of the profit and loss account to the extent that they are no longer of value. And while under FRS3 it is possible to find information on the tax and minority implications of disposals in the notes to the accounts, that information need only be given where practicable.

Table 1 – Under FRS3

	1992	1991
	(£)	(£)
Operating profit	160m	140m
Business disposals	10m	–
Interest	(40m)	(40m)
Pre-tax profit	130m	100m
Taxation	(25m)	(30m)
Profit after tax	105m	70m
Minority interests	(10m)	(5m)
Profit after tax and minorities	95m	65m
Earnings per share	9.5p	6.5p

Table 2 – Under SSAP6

	1992	1991
	(£)	(£)
Operating profit	160m	140m
Interest	(40m)	(40m)
Pre-tax profit	120m	100m
Taxation	(55m)	(30m)
Profit after tax	65m	70m
Minority interests	(25m)	(5m)
Profit after tax and minorities	40m	65m
Extraordinary items	55m	–
	95m	65m
Earnings per share	4p	6.5p

Table 3 – Double Disclosure Approach

	1992	1991
	(£)	(£)
Operating profit	160m	140m
Disposals of land, buildings, investments and businesses		
Profits	70m	–
Losses	(60m)	–
Interest payable	(40m)	(40m)
Profit on ordinary activities before tax		
Trading	120m	100m
Disposals	10m	–
	130m	100m
Tax on profit on ord activities	(25m)	(30m)
Profit on ord activities after tax	105m	70m
Minority interests	(10m)	(5m)
Profit attributable to members of company		
Trading	40m	65m
Disposals	55m	–
	95m	65m
Dividends	(44m)	(40m)
Transfer to revenue reserves	51m	25m
Earnings per share		
Trading	4p	6.5p
Disposals	5.5p	–
	9.5p	6.5p

Table 4 – Five year summary FRS3 presentation

	1992	1991	1990	1989	1988
	(£)	(£)	(£)	(£)	(£)
Operating profit	175m	170m	180m	130m	110m
Net profit or loss from disposals	50m	30m	–	(20m)	10m
Profit before interest	225m	200m	180m	110m	120m
Interest	50m	45m	40m	–	30m
Pre-tax profit	175m	155m	140m	110m	90m
Tax	30m	20m	25m	25m	30m
Minority interests	15m	15m	5m	5m	5m
Profit after tax and minorities	130m	120m	110m	80m	55m
Earnings per share	8.7p	8p	7.3p	6.4p	5.5p

Table 5 – Five year summary SSAP6 presentation

	1992	1991	1990	1989	1988
	(£)	(£)	(£)	(£)	(£)
Operating profit	175m	170m	180m	130m	110m
Interest	50m	45m	40m	–	30m
Pre-tax profit	125m	125m	140m	130m	80m
Tax	60m	55m	60m	55m	20m
Minority interests	30m	25m	20m	15m	5m
Profit after tax and minorities	35m	45m	60m	60m	55m
Extraordinary items	95m	75m	50m	20m	–
Profit after extraordinary items	130m	120m	110m	80m	55m
Earnings per share	2.3p	3p	4p	4.8p	5.5p

The kinds of problem which could arise are demonstrated by the tables which look at both the long- and short-term discrepancies which could arise under the old and new regimes.

Tables one to three illustrate presentations of the same basic figures using FRS3, SSAP6 and what might be described as the Bradfield double-disclosure approach.

The tables assume that in 1992 the company sold a business at a profit of £70 million with no tax or minority implications and closed a business at a loss of £60 million while attracting tax relief of £30 million and with £15 million attributable to minorities.

Using FRS3 the effect is to turn a small net disposal profit of £10 million into a large profit of £55 million after tax and minority interests. But only the £10 million net figure would be visible on the face of the profit and loss account.

Under SSAP6 the entire £55 million would be excluded from the earnings calculation.

Using the Bradfield approach the two components of trading and disposals profits would be separately identified at the attributable level and in the earnings per share figure.

Tables four and five demonstrate how it would be possible for a company which was engaged in a significant disposals programme to flatter its earnings profile over a period using FRS3. Disclosing only the net impact of those disposals gives the impression of steadily rising earnings.

The ASB argues that by reference to more detailed information in the notes and on the face of the profit and loss account investors will be able to make more informed conclusions about the underlying profitability of the business.

However, that argument relies heavily on the assumption that investors will be prepared to explore the notes fully and more importantly abandon the quest for a single headline figure. In that respect Bradfield's concerns have been borne out. The City has steadfastly refused to abandon the earnings per share figure and companies have been ready and willing to lend their support. A proliferation of alternative earnings per share figures has sprung up.

The rules governing this alternative earnings figure are not exactly onerous and therefore a high degree of flexibility is injected into the situation. The ASB says that where a company wishes to present an additional earnings per share calculated on another basis then this should be presented on a consistent basis over time and wherever disclosed be reconciled to the amount required by FRS3. The reconciliation should list the items for which an adjustment is being made and the effect that each has on the calculation. There is also a requirement for the ASB approved version to have at least as much prominence as that afforded to the company's version.

What this means is that a company is given a tremendous degree of control over what it regards as the most appropriate basis by which to judge its performance. There are some restrictions, particularly of consistency, and there is always the reference point of the ASB's version which demands a reconciliation. However, it would allow those companies which are lacking somewhat in the scruples department effectively to reintroduce the extraordinary item.

If by its definition of normalized earnings per share a company were to exclude exceptional items from the calculation then it could recapture the glory days of the extraordinary item by default. Providing investors are prepared to accept a company's definition of normalized earnings then all those items excluded from the calculation begin to have less relevance. The ASB may seek their inclusion but if users put more faith in the company's normalized figure and the FRS3 figure then we are not a great deal further forward.

There is another problem in that if the official definition of earnings per share is regarded as unworkable then any hope of comparability between the performance of different companies fades quite quickly. The reason why the price earnings ratio is regarded as useful is because it is a relative indicator. It can be used to measure how different companies in the same sector are doing. If, however, there is no consistency between companies on the basis of calculation then it immediately begins to distort those comparatives.

There has been some attempt to codify the headline earnings per share figure, most notably by the Institute of Investment Management and Research. Its version excludes, among other things, business disposals. However, there has still been a proliferation of different headline figures.

A further point to bear in mind is that the level of disclosure which the ASB demands in a set of accounts is not always provided by a company when it makes its preliminary announcement of its results. This announcement, which gives the first and quite comprehensive snapshot of how the company has done during the year, is much more closely watched by the press and the stock market than the annual report which is published a few weeks later. So not only is there not a great will for users to move away from the headline figure approach to assessing the company, but neither are there always the tools available at a quite crucial time in the reporting cycle. The company's own normalized earnings per share figure will undoubtedly be accompanied by that demanded by FRS3 but there is rarely any great focus on the reconciliation process.

So while extraordinary items may have been all but abolished there is a danger that the problems they created have not been banished but rather moved to another part of the profit and loss account.

This presentational sleight of hand can be conducted at two levels. FRS3 demands that exceptional items should be included in the appropriate format headings by way of a note unless separate disclosure on the face of the profit and loss account is required to allow the accounts to show a true and fair view. It also requires some exceptional items to be disclosed separately and in particular it identifies profits and losses on the sale or termination of an operation, costs of a fundamental reorganization or restructuring and profits or losses on the disposal of fixed assets.

This provides a company with two opportunities. First there is a decision whether something is exceptional or not. Beyond that there is a question of whether the item should be struck before operating profit or further down the profit and loss account.

An exceptional item which is treated as operational will not need to be necessarily shown on the face of the profit and loss account, although it will require disclosure in the notes to the accounts. The more obvious items such as closure costs will have to be shown on the profit and loss account.

There is therefore a complexity and variety of disclosure emerging which could become dangerous. The common strand, however, is that the exceptional item has become as much an outcast as the extraordinary item. Much as the ASB may want exceptionals included as part of earnings per share for the year there is little sign that its wish is being granted.

More worrying still is that the definition of what constitutes an exceptional item may be stretched beyond the bounds of acceptability. The definition of an exceptional item provided by FRS3 is 'Material items which derive from events or transactions that fall within the ordinary activities of the reporting entity and which individually or, if of a similar type, in aggregate need to be disclosed by virtue of their size or incidence if the financial statements are to give a true and fair view.'

It is a definition, however, which assumes that users of the accounts will be taking a more broadly based view of the figures presented before them. In an environment where exceptional items are by default being excluded from the calculation of earnings per share the definition becomes less relevant.

In essence one of the great creative accounting ruses still remains. The checks and balances which are imposed through greater disclosure only have any effect if users are prepared to take advantage of them. That has so far not been the case.

The reasons are plain to see. The five-year analysis provided by Grand Metropolitan shows the earnings per share figure both before and after exceptional items.

	1989	*1990*	*1991*	*1992*	*1993*
Before exceptional items	23.5p	26.6p	29.0p	28.4p	29.7p
After exceptional items	47.3p	33.1p	10.7p	30.3p	20.0p

When exceptional items are excluded the profile is remarkably consistent, showing steady growth through to 1992 where there is a small downturn before picking up again in 1993.

When exceptionals are included in the calculation the picture is altogether more volatile. A fall of 30 per cent in 1990 is followed by a fall of over 60 per cent in 1991 followed by an increase of nearly 200 per cent in 1992 followed by another fall of over 30 per cent in 1993. Only in 1992 are the before and after exceptional figures within 10 per cent of each other. This is not the kind of record which makes any sense to investors.

There is no doubt that were investors to go behind the figures and refer to a full set of accounts then they would be able to make much more sense of the exceptional items inclusive figures. But if you are making a snapshot comparison over a period of time then that may not be regarded as a relevant exercise.

Research carried out in 1994 by the accounting firm Coopers & Lybrand gives some indication of the fragility of the provisions of FRS3. It looked at 100 sets of accounts concentrating on FT-SE 100 companies and others at the top end of the market capitalization scale.

This research indicated that 71 per cent of companies disclosed one or more exceptional item on the face of the profit and loss account but below the operating profit line. The vast majority of these exceptionals related to what have become known as 'super exceptionals' which include profits or losses on the sale or termination of a business, the cost of a fundamental restructuring or rationalization and profits or losses on the disposal of fixed assets. These were items which might also once have been treated as extraordinary. This represents compelling evidence of the extent of exceptional items which are isolated in the profit and loss account. Only 30 per cent of companies showed exceptional items above the operating profit line. A further 14 per cent showed exceptional items above the line but only in the note to the accounts.

In the early days of the FRS3 era the problems associated with extraordinary items appear to have been transferred to the exceptional item. Certainly the majority of companies recognized the need to make a clear differentiation of their profits before and after exceptional items. Some 54 per cent of companies in the Coopers research disclosed two earnings per share figures. Three companies actually showed three eps figures. There was no clear preferred methodology for calculating the alternative eps figures. Although there was some support for the IIMR approach, adopted specifically by 16 per cent of companies, there was a general lack of clarity. The only common theme was that all the alternative methods of calculating the earnings per share figure excluded the implications of exceptional items.

The extraordinary item is dead. Long live the exceptional item.

2. Income and Expenses

If most individuals drew up their own personal profit and loss account it would be a fairly straightforward matter. Income would be the cash they received and expenses the cash they spent. This is a fairly basic approach to personal finance. A degree of sophistication might be introduced through the judicious use of credit cards but by and large it is cash which remains the yardstick by which people judge their own well-being.

If only it were that simple in the corporate sector. For while it is income and expenses which dominate the profit and loss account there is only a modicum of overlap between the way companies reflect their finances and the way that individuals deal with theirs. There remains a high degree of flexibility in terms of what amounts are actually credited to the profit and loss account as income or debited as expense.

There is perhaps less flexibility for creative accounting on the income side of the profit and loss account but even here there are several possibilities. The degree of flexibility will be influenced considerably by the nature of the business. It is much more difficult, for instance, to manipulate the sales of a supermarket chain which is essentially a cash business than it is to tinker with the turnover attributed to a leasing company where there is usually a much more tenuous relationship between the cash handed over by the customer and the provisions of goods or services.

Central to any creativity in the arena of income is the point at which it is recognized. This is not recognition in the same way that you notice a friend on the other side of the street. In fact it is quite fundamental to the level of turnover or sales which a company will disclose as part of its annual results. The reason why a business does not follow the individual's more simplistic approach to income stems from the fixation with matching costs and revenues. It is accepted that the twelve-month accounting period is an arbitrary period in which to measure a company's performance. As we have already seen whether the natural business cycle is six weeks or six years both companies are still required to report annually. To try to help overcome this fundamental flaw the accounting rules are drafted in a way which allows companies to reflect their results in a manner which is not driven by the erratic nature of cash flows but in a way which is designed to present the financial performance with a smoother and long-term profile in mind.

Once it is accepted that actual cash flows do not present a true and fair view of the company's performance then the door marked creativity is pushed wide open. As long as a company can justify with a degree of reasonableness that its income recognition policy is soundly based then it has *carte blanche* to do pretty much what it likes.

An indication of the kind of flexibility which arises in the field of income recognition can be seen by examining the choices, for instance, which a bed manufacturer has. Assume the beds are made to order and that there is a six-month warranty period during which the bed can be returned and a full refund secured. The income could be recognized at several points in the life of the bed. The earliest reasonable opportunity to take account of the income would be at the point of order. Some would argue that it is a little premature. Indeed the Accounting Standards Board has said in no uncertain terms that this would be entirely inappropriate. But once it has been manufactured then the bed is much closer to the customer and by now the bulk of the costs will have been incurred. However, a more likely time to book the sale will be at the point of delivery or when the invoice is raised. This still overlooks the fact that the customer could still default and if you were working on a genuine cash flow system then the income would only be recognized once the payment had been received and cleared. An argument could still be made for deferring recognition until the six-month warranty has expired, at which point the customer will no longer be able to secure a refund. This would no doubt be regarded as excessively prudent.

The financial impact of the timing decision will be most marked in the first year of trading. Once a company is established then the timing differences begin to sort themselves out. However, the example is indicative of the range of justifiable choices which are available in one simple illustration.

In fact the question of warranty payments is of itself an area which offers some creative accounting opportunities. The way in which a company chooses to deal with them can have a marked impact on the declared income for the year. To start off with there is the debate about whether the warranties should be seen as a reduction in sales or an expense of the business. The financial effect ultimately is the same but the way it is presented can give a rather different impression of the same situation.

Take Companies A and B. Both sell exactly the same numbers of the same product at the same price. Both incur warranty claims amounting to half their sales and the other cost of sales equate to 25 per cent of the gross selling price. Assume sales are £24 million but that Company A treats warranties as a cost of sale while Company B shows sales net of warranties.

Table 7

	Company A	Company B
	(£m)	(£m)
Sales	24	12
Cost of sales	18	6
Gross profit	6	6

The gross profit figure is the same but Company A is making an apparent margin of 25 per cent on sales while Company B is making a 50 per cent margin. Company A looks like a high-volume low-margin business where Company B appears to be operating in high-value-added territory. That could have quite an impact on the perceptions which outside investors have of the two companies. The example is purposely exaggerated but it serves to make the point.

Not only is there flexibility over where in the profit and loss account the warranty payment is declared; there is also a high degree of mobility over the deduction which should be made. Bearing in mind that it is highly unlikely that warranties will reflect actual cash payments or refunds it is therefore up to the company to decide at what rate it would like to make a provision for warranties and when. There is an opportunity here for a company to overprovide when business is booming so that it can either reduce warranty provisions or even write some back when the going gets a little tougher.

The following example gives some idea of the different pictures which can be presented depending on the approach taken to both warranties and income recognition. Two Companies, A and B, make the same product and sell them to the same customer. Company A accounts recognizes sales on

	Year 1	Year 2	Year 3
	(£m)	(£m)	(£m)
Company A			
Sales	12	12	–
Warranties	–	(6)	(6)
Net	12	6	(6)
Company B			
Sales	3	9	6
Warranties	–	(4.5)	(1.5)
Net	3	4.5	4.5

receipt of order. Company B accounts for its sales as 50 per cent on installation and 50 per cent on completion of the warranty period. Each company receives twenty-four orders, one a month for two years, each worth 1 million. It takes six months from the receipt of order to complete an installation and the warranty period is six months. Company A makes no provision for warranties even though half of each order will have a problem and a full refund will then become due.

Over the three-year period both companies have exactly the same net performance with profits in total of 12 million. They are portrayed, however, in very different terms. Company A is quite an erratic animal. After a flying start with net profits four times as large as Company B's it plunges rapidly downhill towards a loss in Year 3. Company B, on the other hand, is an altogether more stable proposition and has a profits profile which is much less volatile.

It can be argued that income recognition is a valuable smoothing tool which allows companies to iron out some of the peaks and troughs of their cash flow profile and to match revenue more evenly with costs. Where the question becomes more troublesome is where companies accelerate the income recognition to an extent where rather than address the mis-matching problem it creates an altogether more sinister and exaggerated kind of mismatching.

This was a technique most prevalent among leasing companies which developed a worrying habit of front loading the income recognized from new leasing agreements. Computer leasing companies would take as income a part of the estimated residual value of a particular piece of hardware. The residual value was deemed to be the amount the leasing company would realize from the sale of the computer, which it owned, at the expiry of the lease period. The figure was particularly arbitrary given the fast-changing nature of techno-logy, and the combination of imprudent residual values together with imprudent income recognition increased the potential for mishap.

On a lesser scale any company which rents out equipment over a long period of time will often charge an installation fee. This will sometimes be taken up front providing a boost to sales rather than spread more evenly across the life of the contract.

This is an issue which has also cropped up more recently in the context of what are known as reverse lease premiums. These are essentially payments made by landlords to encourage a new tenant to take out a lease on a property. During the difficult times the property market went through in the wake of the recession of the early nineties these incentives became commonplace as landlords sought new ways to entice tenants into their buildings. The well-known problems with Canary Wharf in London's Docklands, for instance, have prompted a whole range of attractive incentives designed to draw companies into the development.

Reverse premiums have also been commonplace in the retail sector where problems on the high street led to over supply. In an attempt to encourage shopkeepers to take out long leases significant payments have sometimes been made to prospective tenants.

The matter came to a head in the wake of problems at Pentos which includes the Dillons bookshop chain and Athena the poster shops, and which went into receivership in March 1995.

In its 1993 accounts the company sets out its policy on reverse premiums in the following terms: 'Reverse premiums arising in the period are matched with the costs of negotiating property leases and premia, and the costs of holding and maintaining unused property. The remaining balance of reverse premiums is taken to the profit and loss account over two accounting periods to match the initially low performance of new shops in the start-up period.'

There is nothing wrong with reverse premiums. Indeed a good management will take every advantage of them. The difficulty is that if they are not disclosed properly or if they are taken up front then it can distort the underlying financial position. The matter is being addressed by the Urgent Issues Task Force. It is minded to oblige companies to spread the benefit of the premiums over a longer period, perhaps five years, and is also contemplating improved disclosure.

A more complex question is how to deal with the benefits which arise from the other incentives associated with property. It is not uncommon for new tenants to be offered rent-free periods when they first occupy a building. This is an unsustainable benefit which will have an impact on profitability once a tenant resumes rental payments.

If companies were entirely committed to the concept of matching costs and revenues they would spread these benefits over a longer period by attributing a notional charge for rent even when none was actually being paid.

This is very much an issue for the expenses side of the profit and loss account which is an even more fruitful area for the creative accountant than income. The question of rent-free periods is unusual in that it is rare for a company to receive something for nothing. However, there are numerous other techniques which are available to help keep expenses under control.

There are four basic techniques which crop up time and time again which can help limit the costs that a company reports. Expenses can be capitalized and taken direct to the balance sheet as part of the associated asset. They can be allocated, which is a variation on the capitalization theme and normally involves costs being identified as part of the company's stock. Expenses can be dealt with directly through reserves and most crudely the company simply underprovides for them.

Each technique has its own merits and when used prudently can be quite helpful for a company which is determined to present its financial performance in a manner which is most relevant for its investors. However, there can be problems when companies are a little too cavalier in their attitude. The big problem is that any consistent understatement of expenses will ultimately catch up with the company and create significant difficulties. For while creative accounting can be a very valuable smoothing tool it can never physically pay the bills.

A further problem for the user of a set of accounts is that it can sometimes be difficult to assess to what extent the techniques have been used. Improved disclosure has certainly helped but there are many areas where it is still quite difficult to work out precisely what has been going on and therefore to make any realistic judgement on the financial implications.

One of the most commonly used techniques is the capitalization of costs. This has been particularly prevalent in the area of interest charges where companies have decided, quite legitimately, that the cost of borrowing money to build an asset should be included as part of the overall cost of that asset. The approach is indeed condoned specifically by company law. Some of the supermarket chains have been very active in this field, although as the chapter on fixed assets demonstrates this is not an approach without its problems.

Capitalization does not have to be restricted merely to the time leading up to the construction of a building being completed. This was a policy sometimes seen in the hotel industry where interest charges were capitalized even after a property had opened its doors to the public. A company could argue that because it had not yet reached its full capacity interest should still be capitalized. The period could be for as long as three years on the grounds that this is how long it takes to reach normal profitability.

The benefits to the profit and loss account are considerable particularly if no depreciation is ultimately charged on the completed property. However, it also stacks up problems in that it can lead to the overvaluation of assets which is particularly pertinent in times of falling property prices.

Although interest is perhaps the most commonly capitalized expense it is far from the only cost which is a suitable case for this treatment. Using the hotel example other expenses associated with its construction might also be capitalized. Professional fees associated with the project and any pre-opening and development expenditure might also be rolled up as part of the asset rather than as a charge to the profit and loss account.

Another frequent target for capitalization is research and development expenditure. Development expenditure can be capitalized but not research. Even so, this is more contentious than interest charges since the asset which emerges is less readily identifiable than, for instance, a hotel. Some companies will capitalize only that element of expenditure which is associated with buildings and equipment. Others will only capitalize that portion which can be clearly identified with a specific customer contract and which is therefore recoverable.

Computer software costs also crop up on a regular basis in the capitalization column. Electrocomponents describes its accounting policy in the 1993 accounts in the following terms: 'The cost of major computer software is written off over three years from the date of implementation of the software, the balance being carried forward as a prepayment.'

The company also capitalizes other costs. Pre-trading expenses of major new operations are treated in a similar fashion, being written off over three years from commencement of trade with the balance carried forward as a prepayment.

Electrocomponents sells electrical goods and equipment largely through a comprehensive catalogue and some expenses associated with its preparation are also capitalized. The accounting policy in 1993 states: 'Prior to the issue of a catalogue all related costs incurred are accrued and carried as a prepayment. On the issue of a catalogue these costs are written off over its useful life. Major investments in new catalogue design or composition are written off over the period during which the benefits of those investments are anticipated, such period not to exceed three years.'

The aim here is to align costs more closely with the revenues which will be ultimately earned. Electrocomponents indicates that it will write these costs off over time. So while the profit and loss account is shielded from the initial lumpy expenditure it is not protected completely, since the cost will eventually be charged by way of the annual amortization.

This is constructive capitalization which can be a useful tool for both management and investors. That is not always the case and it can also be used as an implement of deception. Often the victim of this deception is as much the company as it is the investor. An unwitting conspiracy of self-delusion begins with costs being effectively removed from the profit and loss account and transferred to the balance sheet. It appears something of a golden scenario since profits are improved and assets are increased. Yet all it is doing is deferring the problem to a later point in time.

This is a particular danger in the context of cost and overhead allocation. This is a variation of the capitalization theme and occurs most frequently in the context of stock. The rules allow companies to allocate some costs of production to the valuation attributed to stock. It is an area of murky grey and the issue is discussed in more detail in the chapter dealing with stock.

By way of example of how this overhead allocation can go wrong it is worth looking again at the Pentos accounts for 1993. The company states in its accounting policy that the cost of work-in-progress and finished goods includes an appropriate proportion of production overheads and development costs.

There is absolutely nothing wrong with this policy which mirrors that followed by many businesses. However, the note to the accounts which sets out the breakdown of the £56.5 million of exceptional items which contributed to an overall loss for the business of £72.1 million provides some insight into the problems which can arise if the allocation is imprudent.

Some £17.5 million of the exceptional charge relates to the overall cost of sales. The note explains that of this some £10 million relates mainly to labour and overhead recovery in stock, costs of intellectual property rights which are now regarded as irrecoverable, and provisions for slow moving and obsolete costs. In other words the overheads and costs which had been allocated or capitalized had created an overstatement of assets.

As the scale of the losses suggests 1993 was something of a difficult year for Pentos. A new chairman was appointed in the November of that year and a new chief executive was appointed on 1 January 1994. It often takes a new broom to deal with the overhang of earlier accounting policies.

The new management also reversed another allocation policy which had tended to distort the picture the company was presenting to the outside world. Retailing can be quite a seasonal business and what Pentos had been doing was to allocate overheads in accordance with seasonal sales fluctuations. This may have been in keeping with the broad idea of matching costs and revenues but was presenting a picture which was too much out of line with the underlying reality. The original policy which tended to increase profitability in the first half of the year has been reversed and while it will have a significant adverse impact on the company's interim results it will mean that in future the profits and losses will reflect more closely the seasonal nature of the business.

The company also provides a warning about the dangers of the most unsophisticated of methods of keeping expenses out of the profit and loss account. The nature of the business cycle is such that at the year end a company will have received goods and services for which it has not yet been invoiced. The matching principle dictates that these costs must be accounted for and part of the year-end book-closing procedure is to compile a list of these accruals. They are by nature only estimates and therefore capable of manipulation.

It has to be said, however, that the benefits of any manipulation can only be very short-lived. Bearing in mind that the goods or services will have been received it is then only a matter of time before payment falls due. A company may succeed in depressing its expenses in one year only to increase them effectively in the next. The only way that this can be overcome is to make an even bigger underprovision at the end of the second year. Again the problems are being accumulated for the future.

The new management at Pentos clearly realized that there was a problem and again as part of its explanation of the exceptional charges incurred in 1993 it revealed the following: 'The group, in the ordinary course of business, acquires stocks from a very large number of suppliers. The group's assessment of goods received not invoiced at the end of each year is necessarily estimated. The board has this year established more comprehensive procedures for arriving at this estimate and an additional charge of around £7.5 million has been made as a consequence.'

The implication of this is that the company's procedures were inadequate and there was no concerted attempt to underestimate the provision. The effect, however, is the same and Pentos found that it had quite a lot of catching up to do.

In the end there was too much catching up to deal with. Although the management had recognized the accounting problems the extent of the trading difficulties was too great for the new team to grapple with. Receivership was deemed to be the only option. Pentos is a good example of the dangers a company can expose itself to when it allows accounting to mask underlying trading problems.

Underprovisioning is a very short-term technique. It will sometimes be used as a knee-jerk response to a difficult trading year. The creative accountant with a longer-term perspective can ironically use overprovisioning to his advantage. This is dealt with in more detail in the chapter on current assets and liabilities.

Overprovisions can work in two ways. The first is the most constructive since it involves setting aside amounts in the good years a little in excess of the provisions which are actually required. It could be a provision for doubtful debts or indeed for uninvoiced goods received. The charge will depress profits slightly in the good years. When the going gets rough, however, the company can smooth its profits either by running down the excess provision or by topping it up with an amount which is below that which is actually required. It is simple, but effective.

The second approach is less satisfactory since it can only really be used when a company is in trouble. The kitchen sink approach sets up significant provisions covering a broad range of items. The consequence is a very big charge to the profit and loss account. There is no disguising this but the circumstances are such that the City will tend to accept the provisions as a bold attempt by management to restore order to a disorderly company.

Once the provisions are set up they can then be run down. The cash payments are made as they fall due but the charge goes not to the profit and loss account but to the provision which has already been established. The effect is to protect the reported long-term profitability of the business.

The great irony is that sometimes this bold action will be widely applauded. The new management is seen to be getting to grips with the problems and taking firm and decisive action to deal with them once and for all. The new broom is certainly at work but it is never entirely clear whether the problem is being swept away or merely swept under the carpet. There is a danger that the very creation of these provisions persuades the management that there is no longer a problem. Because its effects are not felt on the profit and loss account for two or three years it is therefore regarded as much less of an issue. Its very invisibility makes it hard for anyone to assess how effective the measures are that have been taken. There is one notorious example of a company which set aside big provisions to deal with a loss-making division. It was widely praised for its robust response. Yet it did nothing to address the problem. The continuing losses were merely soaked up in the balance sheet. Three years later it had to make yet more provisions. Little wonder then that the ASB is preparing to attack the whole provisioning mechanism.

This provisioning worked best in the bad old days of extraordinary items when these big charges could be taken below the line and excluded from the earnings per share calculation. In the post-FRS3 climate they must be disclosed as exceptional items and theoretically will hit earnings. As we have seen, however, there is a tendency for exceptionals to be overlooked by the outside world. At least now the effect will form part of a company's long-term accounting record. In the old days the extraordinary item ensured they were shuffled off to reserves never to be heard of again. A company could have been the subject of huge extraordinary items in the past which were soon forgotten about leaving it with a ten-year record which looked extremely impressive.

If expenses are to be taken direct to reserves then the best opportunity remains with the provisions which are made at the time of acquisition. Although the Accounting Standards Board has outlawed these fair value provisions, dealt with in more detail in the chapter on mergers and acquisitions, there will still be some opportunity to create them. This allows a company in effect to take costs of rationalization and restructuring direct to reserves. Once a provision is created, on acquisition, the actual costs are then charged to the provisions rather than against the profit and loss account.

The use of provisions has become commonplace and the big problem this causes for users of accounts is that they weaken the already tenuous relationship between the profit and loss account and cash flow. Companies secure the ability to protect the profit and loss account from costs which would otherwise reduce profitability. Improved disclosure means that it is difficult for companies to hide the larger provisions. However, a considerable amount of tinkering can go undetected.

The problem with capitalization of expenses is that it is hard for investors to assess with any confidence the 'merits of the exercise. There have been a number of examples where the capitalization has produced an over-deferral of expenses which has resulted in a drastic on-off adjustment.

The same difficulties apply to the question of income recognition where it is the basis of the underlying accounting policy which is often more difficult to judge than the policy itself.

The upshot is that on both sides of the profit and loss equation there is considerable departure from the physical cash flow of the business. The very strengths for this departure are also the source of the weakness which is created when the bounds of legitimate flexibility are pushed too far.

Although there remains a quite charming confidence in the certainty of the one figure which identifies a company's profitability for the year it is a confidence which is not always well placed. The necessary room for manoeuvre a company has means that the final profit or loss for the year will not have the precision which is sometimes expected. It is a basis for negotiation and not a great deal more.

3. Foreign Currencies

Although the British are naturally an island race, few companies these days can afford to accept this as a fact of commercial life and take comfort from the reassurance that this provides. Instead, most businesses actively strive to broaden their trading horizons. This involves in its simplest form either exporting finished products or importing goods for reprocessing or onward sales. The more advanced international traders will have subsidiaries and investments based overseas. Whatever the nature and magnitude of a company's international business it will at some stage have to deal with the vagaries of the foreign exchange markets. A transaction which appears quite profitable at one exchange rate will suddenly plunge into loss at another. An overseas investment can have its value eroded as exchange rates change.

The exposure to currency fluctuations is a price that has to be paid for access to international markets. Of course that price can often result in a very welcome refund if exchange rates reverse as they often will. The principle that what goes up must come down even if it does go up again at a later date applies. Clearly the erratic nature of exchange rates is something of a problem. It is yet another uncertainty with which a business has to cope when it is trying to plan its longer-term strategy and assess investment opportunities. In recent years currency movements appear to have become even more frequent and pronounced. As the process of internationalization of capital markets gains momentum the prospects for stabilization become even more remote as the currency speculators take advantage of the new opportunities which will present themselves.

However, it is not just the practical trading uncertainties which pose problems for a company. Some of these can be offset anyway by some judicious hedging. A more lasting difficulty is over how to deal with the surpluses and deficits which arise when overseas assets and liabilities denominated in foreign currencies are translated back into sterling for consolidation purposes. It is a difficulty which has been recognized by the accountancy profession and its rules on how to translate the financial statements of foreign subsidiaries are set out in Statement of Standard Accounting Practice 20. As usual the rules appear to be fairly rigid but in fact offer an element of flexibility.

The basic rules for translating the results of foreign subsidiaries are that a company should use the 'closing rate/net investment' method. This recognizes that the parent's investment is not in the individual assets and liabilities of an overseas company but rather in its net worth. This is represented, in effect, by the equity stake which the parent has in the foreign company's net assets. Under this translation method, the parent should apply the closing rate of exchange, that is the rate in force at the balance sheet date, when translating its net investment in the foreign subsidiary. This process also involves retranslation of the net investment at the beginning of the year at the exchange rate used at the year end. This will normally give rise to an exchange difference, which could be either a profit or a loss. That difference does not have to be reflected in the consolidated profit and loss account but instead is taken direct to the group reserves and disclosed as a movement thereon. Under Financial Reporting Standard 3 those gains and losses, however, now have greater visibility since they must be disclosed in the separate statement of total recognized gains and losses.

The parent must also consolidate the actual trading results of the overseas subsidiary and here the accounting rules permit two different methods of translation. The holding company can choose either to use the closing exchange rate or an average for the year. If it chooses the average rate then this can be calculated on any reasonable basis although it should be weighted to reflect the changes both in the exchange rate itself and the volume of transactions at particular times of the year. It is this option on which rate to use for the translation exercise which presents an immediate creative accounting opportunity, although it has considerable limitations. While it may be advantageous for a company to decide that the time has come for them to switch from using the closing rate to the average rate of exchange for translating the results of overseas subsidiaries this sudden change of heart is not one to be repeated regularly.

The financial effect of that change is best illustrated by a simple example. Take a subsidiary which makes profits of 10 million Draconian Dollars in both 1994 and 1995. The year end translation rates are taken as D$1.1 and D$1.4 respectively to the pound. In 1994 the sterling equivalent of the Draconia profit is around £9.1 million. But at 1995 closing exchange rates the same profit in dollar terms is reduced to a little over £7.1 million, a £2 million fall.

This of course will not go down too well with the company chairman who quite rightly wants to know why reported profits have gone down when in reality they have stayed the same. Long orations on the injustices of the foreign exchange markets are no response to falling profits so enter stage left the average exchange rate. Using the example above and assuming that the average is D$1.2 to the pound, the D$10 million profit then becomes on translation a sterling profit of £8.3 million. It is still a fall but not nearly as exaggerated as the one which is reported using the closing rate.

The arguments which are often presented in defence of the change in the exchange rate used in translation are well rehearsed. The average is more representative of the actual rates ruling during the year. This method reflects more closely the underlying trading performance of the individual subsidiary. The closing rate is rather artificial since it is representative of only one day's dealings in the various exchange markets. This is all true. But the question which must then be asked is, 'If it is so right to use average rates now, why were closing rates used in the first place?' The honest answer is that it made reported profits look that much better.

The translation switch is the most obvious foreign currency ploy used by creative accountants but it is rather crude and one which cannot be repeated too frequently. There is, however, a more subtle tactic which often escapes unnoticed. This relates to the treatment of borrowings, or, in rarer circumstances, deposits. The accounting rules distinguish between short-term money, which falls due within one year of the balance sheet date, and long-term money. The rules for short-term borrowings are that any gains or losses on exchange should be accounted for through the profit and loss account. The short-term nature of the funds should allow the company justifiably to treat the gains as realized and thus there will be no conflict with company law which dictates that only those profits which are realized at the balance sheet date should be included in the profit and loss account.

However, the same cannot be said for long-term borrowings. Clearly, if gains on such borrowings were to be treated as profits then this would conflict with the provisions of company law. The implication of the legal requirements is that any exchange losses would be recognized and accounted for as a deduction from profits for the year, but any gains would have to be excluded until such time as they were realized. This, the accountancy profession says, is illogical and, worse than that, would not comply with the accruals concept. Further, it would also inhibit fair measurement of the performance of the enterprise in the year. For these reasons the accounting standards advocate that exchange gains as well as losses should be recognized in the profit and loss account. This departure from the general rule must be noted in the accounts and specific details of gains and losses relating to each item must be maintained.

That is a small price to pay for the privilege and few companies which have taken advantage of this anomaly would argue with SSAP20, which tells us: 'This symmetry of treatment recognizes that there will probably be some interaction between currency movements and interest rates and reflects more accurately in the profit and loss account the true results of currency involvement.' Quite so.

However, the accountancy profession giveth and the accountancy profession taketh away. For although the standard openly condones and encourages this departure it does temper its incitement to riot with some words of caution on what it calls the exceptional circumstances when the gains have got a little large and there are doubts about the convertibility or marketability of the currency in question. It is up to the company to express those doubts; so effectively it can choose to exclude some element of exchange gains should it so wish, thus allowing it to retain control over the level of reported profit in a particular year which helps to maintain a smooth growth pattern.

The creative accounting opportunities on long-term borrowings do not stop there. Further scope comes in the shape of the treatment of borrowings which have been used either to finance or provide a hedge against foreign equity investments. You will recall that these equity investments must be translated at closing rates of exchange and the differences which arise on the retranslation of the opening net investment at those closing rates are taken directly to and disclosed as a movement on reserves.

The standard permits a similar treatment for those long-term borrowings which were taken out as financing or hedging instruments for the overseas investment. This does not in itself seem particularly outrageous and would appear to make a lot of sense. Isn't the matching of assets and liabilities, after all, sound commercial practice? In situations where this has been the genuine motive for raising the overseas borrowings, so it is. However, this is not always the case. Many companies now raise money overseas purely as a function of effective treasury and risk management. Loan portfolios are becoming increasingly diverse as companies make use of the international capital markets and the ever increasing range of funding instruments which are available. There then comes a problem in identifying which particular loans have been used to finance or hedge against specific overseas investments. The responsibility for that identification rests with the company and it is well within the realms of possibility that Yen denominated loans taken out in Japan could be designated as hedging instruments against an equity investment in the US. Any losses on the translation of the loan into sterling which would otherwise have been deducted from profits for the year can thus be taken direct to reserves and offset instead against the exchange gains on the translation of the equity investment. The opportunities for manipulation are therefore substantial and although the standard insists on consistency of treatment, the year with the next, this will not always be quite so easy to enforce. When borrowings are classified as hedging rather than financing instruments there is little to prevent the company switching into different currencies each year and perpetuating the creativity.

The effect of this flexibility is demonstrated by two companies A and B which both make investments in subsidiaries in Katanga, a small country somewhere in Africa. The net value of both investments at the start of the year is 400 million Katanganese dollars and at that time the exchange rate is 4 to the pound. At the same time as part of their treasury management programme both companies take out borrowings in selected currencies from around the world including a loan in Howhi, a small country in the Far East. Both loans are to the value of 600 million Howhian francs and the exchange rate at the start of the year is 6 to the pound. A year later the net investment in Katanga is unchanged but the exchange rate has slipped to 2 to the pound. The Howhian loan is also unchanged but the rate there at the year end is 4 to the pound. Company A decides that the Howhian loan was a hedge against the investment in Katanga and therefore sets the exchange loss on those borrowings against the gain on the investment. Company B treats the Howhian as a long-term loan and accounts for it accordingly. The impact of the two different treatments on reserves is as follows:

	Company A		Company B	
	(£m)	(£m)	(£m)	(£m)
Opening investment K$400m at 4	100		100	
Closing investment K$400m at 2	200		200	
Exchange gain taken to reserve		100		100
Opening loan HF600m at 6	100		100	
Closing loan HF600m at 4	150		150	
Exchange loss	(50)		(50)	
Exchange loss taken to reserve		(50)		–
Net gain taken to reserves		50		100

The impact on the company profit and loss accounts, assuming that both A and B made profits of £30 million before exchange adjustments and that no tax is payable, is as follows:

	Company A	Company B
	(£m)	(£m)
Trading profits	30	30
Exchange loss	–	(50)
Pre-tax profit/(loss)	30	(20)

The overall effect is highly material. By offsetting its exchange loss on the loan against the non-distributable gains on the overseas investment, Company A has kept its trading profits intact. Company B, however, is faced with a loss for the year which of course would not go down too well with the stock market.

However, there is a further, important discrepancy which relates to the dividend policies which the two companies are able to pursue. Assuming that neither company has sufficient distributable reserves to call on, Company B is unable to make a distribution to its shareholders, another bear point as far as the City would be concerned. Company A, however, has profits in the year which are available for distribution and could duly declare a dividend. Yet that dividend is sourced only because Company A adopted a particular accounting treatment. It is a far from satisfactory outcome for not only is comparability between the two companies drastically impaired but one of them is in a position to embark on a dividend distribution policy which is far from prudent and might in the longer term leave its resources dangerously stretched.

The best that the accountancy profession has to offer on this delicate question is that where a dividend can be paid only because of the offset of an exchange loss on borrowings against a gain on an equity investment, then it may be appropriate to seek legal advice. Some might argue that in these circumstances, psychiatric treatment might be more appropriate.

The illustration is of course an extreme example of the impact of different approaches to currency fluctuations, but it does show that within the morass of translations and conversions which have to be undertaken there is adequate scope for considerable manipulation. The disclosure requirements relating to foreign currency translation and the complex nature of the transactions and their underlying concepts are such that much of the creative accounting will be hidden from public view. It is very difficult for readers of a set of accounts to appreciate, with any degree of certainty, exactly what has been going on.

The obscurity only serves to encourage the use of the techniques which have been outlined above. In general they should only be used for genuine hedging against exchange fluctuations but the arguments for making use of their profit-smoothing propensities are compelling and providing they are applied in moderation should not inflict any lasting damage on the company's underlying financial strength.

The most notable example of how the treatment of foreign currency can distort a company's true underlying performance involved Polly Peck, which is now in the hands of the administrators. The company had extensive interests in Turkey and Northern Cyprus where high rates of inflation were eroding the value of the company's investments. This erosion was reflected not in the profit and loss account but direct to reserves. The 1988 accounts show that retained profit was depleted by £170.3 million in the year as a result of exchange variances on net investments overseas. This came on top of a £35.9 million depletion the previous year. Yet pre-tax profits for the sixteen-month period which ended on 31 December 1988 were just £144.1 million, considerably less than the exchange loss which had been taken direct to reserves.

In effect what Polly Peck was doing was taking credit for profits generated in high-inflation weak-currency areas but not reflecting the sterling cost of financing the working capital which was required. Some estimates at the time of the company's collapse suggested that some 70 per cent of its profits in the previous five years had been eroded by foreign currency losses which were not reflected in the profit and loss account.

The Accounting Standards Board has recognized the problem and is concerned that the rules do not adequately deal with this type of situation. SSAP20 does cover the issue saying that where a foreign enterprise operates in a country which has a very high rate of inflation it may not be possible to present fairly in the historical cost accounts the financial position of a foreign enterprise simply by a translation process. In such circumstances, it says, the local currency financial statements should be adjusted where possible to reflect current price levels before the translation process is undertaken.

Quite how this applies in practice is less clear and the Urgent Issues Task Force has therefore produced its own abstract on how to account for these operations in hyper-inflation economies. This acknowledges that without properly reflecting inflation the company will receive a boost to its profits either from high interest income on deposits in a rapidly depreciating local currency or from trading operations which are showing unrealistically high profitability.

The big problem, however, is in defining what constitutes hyper-inflation. Even when this is done there are still difficulties in finding the right and reliable kind of data which can be used to adjust the local currency operations. The UITF has ruled that adjustments are required where the distortions caused by hyper-inflation are such as to affect the true and fair view given by the group financial statements. In any event adjustments are required where the cumulative inflation rate over three years is approaching or exceeds 100 per cent and where the operations are material. This gives some parameters but there are obviously grey areas which remain.

The UITF identifies two methods of eliminating the distortions. The first is to adjust the local currency financial statements to reflect current price levels; the second is to use a relatively stable currency as the functional currency.

The aim is clearly to force companies to take a more realistic approach towards high inflation in overseas businesses. The problem remains that in the most contentious areas, where inflation is high but not yet in the 100 per cent area or where the operations are not clearly material, there is going to be a degree of debate between the company and the auditor, the outcome of which will depend very much on the final judgements which are taken.

The problems will remain. What is worse from the investors' perspective is that the information they need to make a valid judgement on the implications of foreign currency translation will not always be readily available. Research in 1994 by Company Reporting showed that of 520 annual reports reviewed some 76 per cent showed signs of foreign currency exposure. However, of these only 27 per cent provided any significant detail. In 1991 only 15 per cent of companies gave any significant detail. Clearly there has been some improvement, but there is still a lot to be desired.

Foreign currency will therefore remain an area which will require investors to pay special attention. Where companies take a responsible attitude to the issue and in particular where they recognize the problems of inflation investors have little to worry about. The problem remains, however, that defining responsible is almost impossible.

4. Pensions

One of the most contentious areas of creative accounting in both practical and moral terms relates to pensions. It is therefore an emotive issue and it is not always easy to make the distinctions between the different elements which are part of the great pensions debate. On the one hand there is the question of the pension scheme and its members. They need to know that their rights are secure. They must have clear access to the information which will allow them to establish whether the scheme's trustees are properly securing and managing the assets of the scheme. On the other hand there is the question of how the company itself accounts for the costs of providing the pensions which are promised by the scheme.

The distinction between the two elements is sometimes blurred. It is easy when in a detached frame of mind to see how accounting for the costs of pensions is very different from securing the assets of the fund. However, those who see things in a less technical light can be forgiven for confusing the issues.

The creative accountant has no need to blur the distinction in order to pursue his craft. There is plenty of scope for manipulation of the accounting cost without straying into territory which is altogether more dangerous. While the standard setters therefore pose no threat to pensioners they have not done a great deal to improve clarity of accounting.

The source of this uncertainty is Statement of Standard Accounting Practice 24 which was published by the old Accounting Standards Committee in 1988; it has yet to be revisited by its successor body although this is very much on the agenda. The standard is by nature quite broadly based in that it is designed to apply to all pension schemes irrespective of their size or structure. It is also inherently complex because of the intricacies of the underlying pension assumptions.

SSAP 24 was an attempt to make some sense of an area where it had become increasingly difficult for investors to assess quite what the financial implications of the pension fund were for a given company. This required the introduction of intricate mental and accounting gymnastics and it is perhaps not surprising, therefore, that the standard has not always provided the clarity which had been hoped for.

At the root of its shortcomings is the basic assumption that the pension fund is in effect 'owned' by the company. The use of inverted commas here is important because SSAP 24 does not actually go that far. It does, however, rely for much of its coherence on recognition of the principle that the company is responsible for deficits arising on the fund and is therefore entitled to take account of any surpluses which arise. This stops short of arguing that the fund is no longer distinct from the company and should therefore be recognized in the company balance sheet but it is certainly a step in that direction. This has become particularly contentious in the context of some of the large pension surpluses which have been run up. It could be argued that these should be the property of the members but SSAP 24 says that it is the company which should account for them. In most cases this also brings a benefit to the company either in the shape of a stronger balance sheet, improved profits or both.

This is something of a question of morality but it is not one, for the time being, to trouble those whose job it is to prepare a set of accounts. Their task is not to question the basis of the standard but to comply with its requirements.

Those requirements are drafted in a way which allows a considerable degree of flexibility. So while SSAP 24 has succeeded in bringing some much needed focus to the area it is questionable whether it has done anything to improve the clarity of financial reporting. It is hard to see how comparability between different companies has been improved and it remains, depite improved disclosure, difficult for investors to assess the implications of the pension fund question for the company itself.

The main objective of SSAP 24 is for a company to recognize the cost of providing pensions on a systematic and rational basis over the period in which it receives the benefits of the employee's service. This was a quite radical departure from the previous method where companies had largely just accounted for the pensions costs on the basis of the cash payments made to the fund. It had the beauty of simplicity but it meant that the costs were subject to quite violent fluctuations.

This created no problem for defined contribution or, as they are sometimes known, money purchase schemes since the employer has no obligation beyond those contributions which are set out under the terms of the fund. The charge to the profit and loss account will be simply the annual cost of those contributions.

Altogether more problematic, however, is the accounting for defined benefit or final salary schemes. Here the employer's liability is open-ended and in order to comply with SSAP 24 it becomes necessary to become embroiled with a whole range of actuarial valuations and assumptions. The aim here is to establish a regular charge which should be made to the profit and loss account for the pension cost. However, SSAP 24 introduces the concept of making adjustments to that basic regular cost in order to account for the variations which crop up from time to time.

The regular cost is defined as the consistent ongoing cost recognized under the actuarial method used. Roughly translated this means the level of contributions which the actuary would regard as sufficient to ensure that pensions for future service could be paid out of the scheme providing the current assumptions about the future hold good. Despite the injection of actuary speak this is relatively straightforward as long as you do not get too bogged down in the intricacies of the actuarial assumptions.

More difficult, however, is the concept of variations from regular cost which SSAP 24 insists must be reflected in the accounts. The standard identifies four categories of variations from regular costs. These can be characterized in simple terms. The variations will either relate to changes in the actuarial process, methods and assumptions or they will be a function of changes to the scope or terms of the scheme.

The most frequent variations, and certainly those which have caused the most controversy, relate to changes in the underlying assumptions about the fund which result in either a deficit or a surplus. Very few companies make a song and dance about their deficits so it has been the treatment of pension fund surpluses which has provoked the greatest interest. This is entirely understandable if for no other reason than that under SSAP 24 they have provided a benefit to the company which is outside the normal scope of their business and as some have argued, a benefit to which they are not properly entitled.

These surpluses arise when the actuarial valuation of the fund is greater than its expected liabilities. This is a function of a number of factors, most notably the level of investment returns and the level of wage increases. When returns outpace wage inflation, as they did during the eighties, a surplus can arise. When this is put alongside the sharp reduction in workforces in the recessions of both the early eighties and early nineties then the surplus is accelerated since during those periods the total wage bill was shrinking.

The notion of a company taking advantage of its pension fund surplus was first raised during the mid eighties most notably by Lucas. It was able to announce that it intended to take a pensions holiday which had the effect of boosting pre-tax profits by around £40 million over a two-year period. The announcement also sent the share price soaring which further increased the surplus since the pension fund had a sizeable investment in the company itself. Other companies were following suit and SSAP 24 was therefore intended in part to codify the approach which should be taken.

The basic rule it introduced was for all variations from

regular pension cost, including surpluses, to be spread forward over the remaining service life of employees rather than to be recognized immediately.

An alternative to this approach is permitted whereby at the time of first compliance with SSAP 24 the surplus or deficit can be dealt with as a prior year adjustment. This creates a prepayment on the balance sheet to account for a surplus. An accrual would be established when there is a deficit on the fund.

Year	Amortization method			Prior year & prepayment method		
	Charge	Funding	Provision	Charge	Funding	Prepayment
	(£m)	(£m)	(£m)	(£m)	(£m)	(£m)
Prior year				160		160
1	34	30	(4)	50	30	140
2	34	30	(8)	50	30	120
3	34	30	(12)	50	30	100
4	34	30	(16)	50	30	80
5	34	30	(20)	50	30	60
6	34	30	(24)	50	30	40
7	34	30	(28)	50	30	20
8	34	30	(32)	50	30	–
9	34	50	(16)	50	50	–
10	34	50	–	50	50	–

There is no guidance given by the standard on which of the two methods is preferred. The choice will depend very much on the company's own requirements. The first option will benefit the profit and loss account since the surplus will be amortized over a number of years and therefore reduce the annual charge. The second method will boost the balance sheet so while the profit and loss account will reflect the regular cost of pension contributions the balance sheet is boosted by the presence of a prepayment.

The chosen approach will produce quite different results as the very simple example provided by Ernst & Young on page 44 suggests. It assumes that the company has a surplus of £160 million, the average service life is ten years and that the surplus should be eroded by reducing the regular funding charge from £50 million to £30 million for eight years. The charge to the profit and loss account under the amortization method is calculated by dividing the surplus (£160 million) by the average service life (ten years) and deducting this amount of £16 million from the regular cost of £50 million. No account is taken of interest or the time value of money.

The two methods provide very different presentations of the same situation in the company's accounts even though the funding requirements, which represent the actual cash flow payments, are exactly the same. Under the amortization method the company sees a much lower charge to the profit and loss account since the variation from the regular payment is reflected in the cost. It also builds up a provision which is not reduced until the actual funding payments pick up again to £50 million. Under the prepayment method, however, the annual charge remains at the regular cost of £50 million throughout the period and the big prepayment, which boosts the balance sheet, is steadily eroded.

Already it is plain to see how confusing all this can be for investors and this is before any allowance is made for the real world. Nothing in the magical world of pensions is ever that simple. Once reality is taken into account there will be occasions where a company which adopted the amortization will also receive a boost to its balance sheet. By the same token a company which chose the prior year adjustment approach may also receive benefits for the profit and loss account.

The key here is the account which should be taken of the notional interest which accrues on the deficit or, more importantly, the surplus. The rules are unclear on the subject and essentially it is up to the company to decide whether or not the carrying amount in the balance sheet should reflect notional interest.

This is of most relevance to those companies which choose the prepayment approach since the initial figure in the accounts can be quite large. However, it is also relevant to those companies which select the amortization approach particularly where there is a sizeable surplus. The example above uses a company where the charge to the profit and loss account exceeds the actual amount paid into the fund which gives rise to a provision. In many cases the surpluses will be so large that a charge becomes a credit to the profit and loss account which will also give rise to a prepayment.

There are considerable benefits to be had then for companies with pension funds that are in surplus. Just one item, which a few years ago was never regarded as anything other than untouchable, can now influence, sometimes quite significantly, a company's reported profits, its interest charge, its assets, liabilities and tax charges. Just how significant the impact can be is demonstrated by the note to the Williams Holdings 1993 accounts. It says:

> The pension fund prepayment of £129.3m (1992 £123.5m), which substantially arose in respect of acquisitions, has been included in debtors. The amount represents the surplus arising on implementation of SSAP 24, adjusted for acquisitions and disposals, and subsequent credits to the profit and loss account. In previous years a net pension credit has arisen in the profit and loss account since the interest accrued on the surplus, and the spread forward of the further surplus arising from the actuarial valuation in 1991 exceeded the regular cost of providing pension benefits. To recognize the effect of the ACT changes announced in the 1993 Finance Act, and in advance of the triennial valuation due in April 1994, no credit has been assumed in 1993. The net pension credit in 1992 was £5.7 million.

In Williams' case the advantage of adopting the prior year adjustment approach has been directed more towards the balance sheet although there has clearly been a benefit to reported profits.

Those companies selecting the amortization approach will weight the benefit more in favour of the profit and loss account. The 1994 Courtaulds accounts set out quite clearly the benefits to its profits. The following information is provided under the heading 'Principal pension figures included in the accounts'.

	1994	1993
	(£m)	(£m)
UK scheme		
Regular cost	12.6	12.7
Variation from regular cost	(11.0)	(15.7)
Other schemes	10.5	10.3
Charge to operating profit	12.1	7.3
Credit to interest payable	(11.0)	(18.3)
	1.1	(11.0)
Prepayments included in debtors being excess of pension credits to profit and loss account over amounts funded	42.4	33.4

The operating profit benefits to the tune of £11 million courtesy of the variation from regular cost. The interest charge is reduced by £11 million because of the notional amount arising on the pension surplus and the balance sheet also benefits through an increased level of prepayments.

More relevant perhaps than all this is a further note to the accounts relating to a pension fund repayment. It reads: 'Following the unanimous agreement of the Trustees of the main Courtaulds UK Pension Scheme to a package including improved benefits for members, £49 million (net of £32.6 million tax) was repaid by the scheme to the company on 31 March 1993; the final portion of the repayment amounting to £1.7 million (net of £1.2 million tax) was received in 1993/94 after completion of the valuation.'

This is significant. For many companies the tinkering with the charges for pension funds and the consequent implications for the accounts is entirely unrelated to cash flow. Indeed SSAP 24 is keen to make the distinction between funding requirements and accounting requirements. This is one of the great worries for those whose job it is to assess how a company is doing. The benefits to the profit and loss account and the balance sheet can be considerable yet they only arise as a consequence of the inaccuracy of previous actuarial estimates and themselves are based on another set of estimates which could be equally fallible. Doubts therefore arise as to the quality of the assets or earnings benefits attributable to pension cost accounting.

In Courtaulds' case, however, the surplus has been translated into a tangible benefit to cash flow and is indeed recorded as such. This is relatively unusual since for a fund to part with cash is something of an irrevocable decision. It is one thing to allow a company to benefit from the fund's performance; it is something else to hand over tangible assets.

The confusion is therefore building. There is not just the question of which accounting option to select in the first place; there is also an issue of the ultimate relationship with underlying cash flow which has to be of relevance.

But the confusion about the presentation is nothing once you begin to delve into some of the underlying assumptions which are used in coming to the figures which are disclosed in the accounts. There is no doubt that SSAP 24 has improved the investor's ability to learn more about the reported implications. It does little, however, to help in assessing whether the crucial judgements which underpin the reported figures are appropriate.

The potential problem areas are considerable. Even without getting too bogged down with the actuarial process there are still plenty of grey areas which influence the ultimate accounting outcome.

How, for instance, does a company establish the remaining service lives of current employees? This is the important benchmark for determining the period over which a surplus should be amortized. Some allowance must be made for changes to the workforce. People will retire, they will die, they will leave the company and they will leave the pension scheme. All these factors have to be considered in order to establish a figure for remaining service life. That figure will normally be a lot shorter than some might imagine and will sometimes be less than ten years and rarely much more than fifteen. This figure is critical in calculating the variation from regular cost yet it is based on assumptions. Although these assumptions are very carefully worked through by the actuarial profession they are still only assumptions. Because it relies so heavily on judgements it becomes very difficult for the auditor to disagree with the final conclusion. It does, however, lead to a high degree of inconsistency even between companies in the same sector. In the media sector the range of service lives has been as wide as eight to fifteen years.

Another area offering a high degree of flexibility is the chosen method of amortization for the surplus once it has been identified. The standard does not specify a precise method and there are a wide number of possibilities. The simplest approach is to use a straight line amortization where the same amount is charged each year. But if the average approach to the remaining service lives is not used, the amortization charge will be linked to the specific timings of departures from the pension scheme. This will tend to produce a declining amortization charge but spread over a longer period. As a refinement of this some allowance can also be made for salary inflation which will alter the charges yet again. If interest is also taken into account then the numbers involved will increase significantly. It is quite easy to envisage a whole range of different charges all dealing with the same initial surplus.

At two levels, then, the company, often in consultation with its actuaries, has the ability to influence the charge or credit which appears in the profit and loss account. The problem is compounded in that there is an interrelationship between the estimate for remaining service lives and the amortization method which is chosen. Yet very little of the process which underpins the ultimate charge in the profit and loss account is shared with the user of financial reports. There may be much better disclosure but it remains hard to establish whether that which is disclosed is appropriate or indeed of any relevance.

With further complications arising where there is a significant reduction of employees and when dealing with the pension schemes of acquired companies, to say nothing of the intricacies of dealing with hybrid, foreign or unfunded schemes, it is easy to see why this is an area which is fruitful for the creative accountant and dangerous for the user.

The only comfort for investors is that disclosure has been improved but as we have seen this does not always result in any better understanding of the situation. There is also a danger that investors are inadvertently misled because of the range of different factors which are involved in the process. Very often when companies refer to the benefits of pension credits they will talk about a single net figure. This is entirely reasonable except that it tends to understate the benefit. If a credit of £30 million is offset by a regular charge of £10 million the company may simply talk, when discussing the figures with analysts or the press, about a net credit of £20 million. This can easily be mistaken as being the benefit to the profit and loss account of the surplus. In fact the true benefit is £30 million because without the credit the company would have had a charge of £10 million.

It is an understandable misunderstanding but an important one. Not only is a notional benefit arising but that notional benefit is sometimes being understated. Part of the explanation comes from the enormous complexities surrounding the whole area. Given that it is virtually impossible to make any independent judgement on the pension figures used in a set of accounts users are driven towards relying even more heavily upon the management.

If there is a message for investors it is to treat the issue with great suspicion. The further an item strays away from underlying cash flow the less reliable it becomes. In this case the rules positively encourage that departure which should make users doubly suspicious.

From the company perspective pensions represent an apparent land of milk and honey in abundance. But there is a danger that the illusions can begin to take over from reality. The company, even more than the investor, needs to be wary of any mismatch between reported profits and cash flow.

It is an area which the ASB will return to. It is conscious of the problems which exist. It may well be that the time is approaching where the ASB has to target its thinking as much to the actuaries as the accountants. As we have seen the underlying assumptions can have a significant influence on the figures used in the accounts. The question arises of whether some of these assumptions could be standardized. Why, for instance, does there have to be a range of estimates for British inflation. The fact is that whatever the actual rate is it will be the same for every company. Why then should there be any difference when the rate is a forecast rather than the actual outturn. You will never be able to standardize all the assumptions but some of the main ones could be brought quite easily into line.

Pensions will continue to remain a sensitive and contentious area and not just in an accounting context. When you begin to meddle you are entering dangerous territory.

5. Stock

Stock is the item that perhaps most explicitly affects both a company's balance sheet and its profit and loss account. This privileged position makes it potentially the most important aspect of a company's business and this is reflected in the sleepless nights and sweaty palms which bedevil auditors whenever they have to deal with it. The audit of stock is undertaken with the same fear, care and apprehension which is normally found among bomb disposal experts. There is always this worry that the value attributed to the stock will blow up in the auditor's face taking him and the company with it.

That concern is not without justification. The margin for error is vast. And the errors can be caused for innumerable reasons. It may be straightforward creative accounting, it may be simply unintentional and can also be the function of total malice aforethought. The problem is compounded by the fact that the nature of stock and hence its valuation varies widely from company to company and from industry to industry. It is hard to imagine a farm's stock sharing much in common with that of an advertising agency. Yet both types of business will have an item in their accounts relating to stock and work in progress. It is little wonder that when the Accounting Standards Committee launched its standard on how to deal with the subject in 1975 it was moved to say: 'No area of accounting has produced wider differences in practice than the computation of the amount at which stock and work in progress are stated in financial accounts.' Two decades later nothing has happened to change that position.

It follows then that the scope for creative accounting is extensive. However, it will vary depending on the nature of the company's operations. This chapter therefore deals with the underlying principles involved rather than the specific practices which will be appropriate in one industry but perhaps not in another. For the same reason no analysis is provided of the special circumstances which relate to long-term contract work in progress which is found mainly in the construction industry. Still, the basic themes which underpin creative accounting in the area of stock and work in progress are common to all industries and should provide a sufficient overview for preparers and users of accounts alike to establish the key areas to which attention should be paid.

At this stage it is useful to examine just what the accounting and legal requirements relating to stock are. The basic rule is that stock should be valued at the lower of cost or net realizable value. Company law dictates that a business may use a variety of methods in arriving at the purchase price or production cost of stocks. However, if this value is materially different from the replacement cost of those stocks then this and the amount should be disclosed. Cost, according to the accounting rules, is 'the expenditure which has been incurred in the normal course of business in bringing the product or service to its present location and condition. This expenditure should include, in addition to cost of purchase, such costs of conversion as are appropriate to that location and condition.' It is this last part of the definition which presents the real creative accounting opportunities.

Those three little words 'costs of conversion' mean so much. It is they which allow a company to include as part of its stock valuations an element of production overheads. This of course requires an arbitrary system of allocation which effectively permits the company to charge, within reason, whatever it likes to its stock account. This is particularly important at the year end. The effect is not just to boost the value of the asset recorded in the balance sheet but also to increase profits for the year. This is illustrated by a simple example. Two companies,

A and B, in the same business both have annual sales of £100 million. Both have the same opening stock and purchases of material in the year but put different values on the closing stock. The cost of those sales is thus opening stock of £10 million plus the purchases during the year of £50 million less the closing stock which Company A values at £20 million and Company B values at £15 million. The effect of the different value attributed to the year end stocks is as follows:

	Company A		Company B	
	(£m)	(£m)	(£m)	(£m)
Sales		100		100
Less cost of sales				
Opening stock	10		10	
Purchases	50		50	
Closing stock	(20)		(15)	
		40		45
Gross profit		60		55

Company A turns in a profit £5 million better than that achieved by Company B simply by inflating the value of the year end stock. It will also have the benefit of an additional £5 million of assets in its balance sheet because the attributable cost of the stock will still be less than the net realizable value when it is sold off as a finished product. Yet this anomaly is fairly typical of the kind of problem which is difficult to avoid when arbitrary assessments and judgements are applied in order to arrive at some kind of valuation.

It is testimony to the complexity of the issue that there are so many possible valuation methods. As an illustration here are some, and the word *some* should be stressed, of the approaches used in practice: first in first out, weighted average cost, base stock, specific indexation, next in first out and latest purchase price. In out, in out, shake it all about, you do the year end stock take and you change the sums, that's what it's all about. With such a wide variety of choices available it is hardly surprising that stock valuations sometimes seem to be carried out with the same sense of order as a rather drunken version of the hokey-cokey.

As long as a company can demonstrate that a particular method is the most appropriate for its operations and activities then there is little to prevent its use. In practice the accountancy profession prefers to limit companies to a choice between the first in, first out method of stock valuation and the weighted average price method. Even this limited choice still throws up a wide variation in the resulting valuations.

Companies A and B again have the same opening stocks with the same value, make identical purchases in the year and have the same number of units in stock at the year end. Company A uses the weighted average method of calculating its year end stock value while Company B adopts the first in, first out approach. The details of the stock transactions are as follows:

	Units	Value (£)
Opening stock	200	1,000
Purchases		
January	100	600
March	50	400
June	200	2,000
August	100	1,300
December	150	1,700
Year end stock	350	?

Company A using the weighted average method would value year end stock by pricing each unit at that time at the average cost of units purchased in the year and held at the start. That average price was £8.75 (800 units costing £7,000) which gives a total valuation for year end stock of £3,062.50 (350 units at

£8.75). Company B using the first in first out method values its year end stock on the basis that it is the latest purchases which remain in stock at the year end. The value attributed is therefore that relating to the cost of all the August and December purchases plus half that of the June consignment. This gives a stock valuation of £4,000 (£1,700 + £1,300 + £1,000).

Even from this simple example it is immediately apparent that the two methods bring widely differing stock valuations. Company B's stock is valued at nearly one third higher than that of Company A's yet both businesses have had exactly the same transactions in the year at the same prices and have ended up with exactly the same stock levels. This discrepancy is caused by the fact that the example assumes that the cost of the purchases has been rising in the year. If the prices had remained constant throughout the year then there would have been no difference in the stock valuations irrespective of the measurement method adopted. It follows that if a company wants to carry forward a higher year end stock value then the first in, first out method should be used in times of rising prices and the weighted average method in times of falling prices.

The onus is on the management to adopt a method of stock valuation which is a realistic approximation to the actual costs incurred. The company auditor would expect the method to be regularly reviewed and although eyebrows might be raised if changes to the policy used were instituted on a fairly regular basis simply to take advantage of price fluctuations there is still a substantial element of flexibility. It is only when a company tries to take more than its fair share of unrealized profit by valuing stocks at replacement cost in times of rising prices that the auditors start to get a little worried. Ironically, the requirement of the Companies Act that material differences between the stated stock valuation and its replacement cost be disclosed, is almost an incentive for a company to use the higher valuation, although stocks might then be reported at a higher amount than their actual cost.

However, these methods only relate to the value which is attributable to the cost of the purchases the company makes.

The accounting rules, you will recall, also insist that costs of conversion be included as part of the year end stock. It is the allocation of these overheads and other production costs which give rise to considerable scope for manipulation of the reported stock. There are two main problems. The first relates to the identification of those overheads which are genuinely part of the cost of conversion of the stock. The second is concerned with the suitability of the costing systems which a company uses in order to arrive at a realistic apportionment of the overheads.

Some costs and overheads are immediately identifiable as being directly related to the process of converting bought-in stocks into a state where they are suitable for onward sale or processing. Direct labour costs, direct production expenses and the fixed production overheads are clearly all part of the conversion process. Similarly, costs relating to the supervision and management of production, quality control expenses and items such as insurance, rates and depreciation can be justifiably treated as part of the costs of conversion. The problems arise with the allocation of central costs and overheads which are not obviously linked to production. It could be argued for instance that the company's general management team, particularly in smaller organizations, is actively involved in supervising the production process and therefore an element of the related costs should be attributed to year end stock as part of the costs of conversion. The same problem will arise with central service departments such as the accounts or personnel sections.

The basic rule is that overheads should be classified according to their distinguishing characteristics. The salary of the production manager is therefore a cost of production while that of the marketing manager is not. However, it is obvious that there are many overheads where that distinction is far from clear and it is in these grey areas that some subtle manipulation of the stock figure can be carried out. It is only at the year end that the problem arises since this is when the stock is being carried forward, taking an element of effectively deferred expenditure with it. The cost is not avoided altogether since the closing stocks in one year are of course the opening stocks of the next and will therefore be included as part of that year's cost of sales.

There is another identification problem relating to overheads. This centres on the distinction between what are normal and what are abnormal costs. The accounting rules on stock conversion and valuation are designed to recognize only the usual recurring costs of production. Any costs which are incurred as a result of one-off incidents or events should not strictly be accounted for as part of the conversion process but charged separately to reflect their exceptional nature. So if a batch of stock is accidentally spoiled because of a mishap in the workshop that cost should be strictly written off straight to the profit and loss account rather than included in the stock valuation. Again, though, the decision on whether something is a normal part of the production process or a one-off event is arbitrary in nature. The lack of any hard and fast rules therefore makes it quite easy for a rather liberal overhead allocation policy to be adopted.

The effect of different approaches to the apportionment of overheads on reported profits can be large. Take the identical companies A and B with financial years ending on 31 December. Both have annual sales of £100 million, opening stocks of £30 million and a cost of sales before allowing for year end stocks of £50 million. The closing stocks are valued at £20 million before the allocation of certain central overheads and the cost of an accidental batch spoilage shortly before the year end. The central overheads amount to £24 million in the year. Company A allocates a part of these to the production process and estimates that the December costs of £2 million should be attributed to closing stock. Company B charges the central overheads to the profit and loss account as they are incurred. Similarly Company A includes the batch spoilage, which cost £5 million, as a cost of conversion and thus in its year end stock. Company B writes the spoilage off straight to the profit and loss account. The trading statements of the two companies are as follows:

	Company A		Company B	
	(£m)	(£m)	(£m)	(£m)
Sales		100		100
Less				
Opening stock	30		30	
Costs of sales	50		50	
Closing stock	(27)		(20)	
		(53)		(60)
Gross profit		47		40
Less				
Central overheads	22		24	
Stock spoilage	–		5	
		(22)		(29)
Net profit		25		11

The effect in this particular year is quite startling. Company A comes out with net profits which are more than twice those earned by Company B. It also carries in the balance sheet stock which is valued at £7 million more than Company B's. This discrepancy is merely a function of the different treatments of overheads.

However, do not forget that this stock valuation will catch up with Company A in the following year. Its profits will at the outset be £7 million behind those of Company B and therefore Company A will have to deter even more overheads in that year if it is to make up the difference. This knock-on effect cannot be ignored. It is easy sometimes to overlook this factor and a company must take into account the longer-term considerations when assessing its overhead allocation policy. However, as a means of making up for a short-term decline in trading which can be made up in the following year then a clever use of overhead allocation can be very effective.

For companies where the business does not have a production process then the scope for manipulation might be more restricted. Even so, central overheads are a common feature in all businesses and therefore there is some room for manoeuvre when they are allocated.

More important, a company, and therefore its shareholders, should be aware of the opportunities which overhead allocation offers for smoothing out those unwanted profits fluctuations. This is by far and away its best use as a creative accounting tool. Any abuse will only put undue pressure on the trading performance of future years and will ultimately exasperate the company's auditors unnecessarily.

The difficulty with the allocation of overheads is not just related to a proper identification. Confusion can also be generated by the cost and overhead absorption system which the management uses. There are countless systems which are generally categorized as aspects of management accounting. A whole range of budgetary controls and variance analysis systems might be employed. Be they standard cost, marginal cost, full cost or zero-based budgeting systems the purpose is essentially to allow the management some degree of control over the expenses of production. These systems are too complex and too varied in their nature to explore in any detail. However, each will be subject to the same type of uncertainty which arises when the assumptions on which the systems are based become no longer appropriate. This can lead to distortions and discrepancies which the accountancy rules are keen to avoid. These dictate that the system which is used as the basis for overhead allocation to year end stocks should be based on the company's normal level of activity. Some managers may argue that there is no such thing as a normal level of activity but the accountancy profession does not let things like that stand in the way of a sound and solid principle.

If the company's management is not entirely sure what is meant by the normal level of activity then there are a number of suggestions available to help them out. As a starting point some attention might be paid to the volume of production which was intended by the designers, and, indeed, the management, when the facilities were first set up, given the working conditions and shift system which prevailed during the year.

This is a fine idea in principle but the intentions when a factory was first built or a workshop set up might well have been overtaken by events outside the company's control which have resulted in a reassessment of the position. To cope with this the appendix to the accounting standard dealing with stocks suggests that attention should also be paid to the budgeted levels of activity for the year under review and ensuing years. Attention should also be paid to the levels of activity which are actually achieved in the year and how this compares with previous years. All this attention is being paid with such studious care for one simple purpose – to make sure that any unused capacity is written off in the year it wasn't used.

As many companies have found to their cost, they are positioned in industries which still suffer from overcapacity. Clearly this has very serious long term implications for the viability of the individual companies and in some cases, the industry itself. However, it also poses some short-term problems in how to account for the overheads which relate to the unused element of a company's capacity. The extent of the difficulty is easy to see if you imagine a fixed overhead of £100 which relates to a production line which is designed to make 100 units a year when operating at full capacity. The attributable overhead is £1 a unit. However, if the company's business suffers and the production line only operates at half capacity, the 50 units produced then attract an overhead of £2 a unit, double that under full capacity. The question then arises as to whether the extra £1 should be carried forward as part of the year end stock valuation or written off as a cost for the year.

Clearly the answer will affect the stock valuation and of course reported profits for the year. On the same principle, which was demonstrated in the overhead identification example, the more overhead which is included in stock the higher its value and the higher the profits for the year. It is always going to be difficult to form a firm conclusion on what is represented by normal activity and therefore the best that the company's auditors can hope for is that they will be able to form a view on the chosen system's reasonableness. That reasonableness offers enormous potential for manipulation.

There are two main thrusts to the creative accounting which can be carried out in this area. The first, which is perhaps more limited, is to toy around with the company's normal operating capacity. By assuming a lower level of activity than is anticipated a company will be able to attribute a higher level of overheads to each item of stock which could assist in boosting the year end stock valuation. The drawback with this is that the company's auditors are likely to insist on some element of consistency in the view which is taken on what constitutes normal activity. The accounting rules quite graciously acknowledge that there are such things as variances and short-term fluctuations but they do not tolerate habitual offenders. Although temporary changes in the load of activity may be ignored, persistent variations should lead to a revision of the previous norm. This may give the company sufficient flexibility to overcome its own short-term problems but it does limit the opportunities to repeat the tactic at a later date.

A better method of tampering with the year end stock valuations is to manipulate the actual level of manufacturing operations. These can be speeded up or slowed down towards the year end, or the time of the annual stocktaking if this takes place at a different time, in order to influence the physical levels of stock which a company has at the year end. This is perhaps more an example of creative management than creative accounting but the effect is still the same. The stock position at the end of the company's year is artificially inflated or deflated. It may be particularly appropriate for those companies which, because of tight year end reporting deadlines imposed by an overseas parent, have to carry out a physical check before the end of the year and then adjust forward for the outstanding months.

Again, it must be remembered that excessive abuse of the overhead allocation system can eventually catch up with a company. However, some judicious management and careful allocation of the relevant costs can help enormously in the profits smoothing process. The same is true of the attitude which is taken to any inefficiencies in the production process. The position here is similar to that of the one-off incidents such as the stock spoilages mentioned in the example on overhead identification. Once again there is an incentive for a company to include the cost of any production inefficiencies in the year end stock valuation rather than to write them off in the year in which they occurred. The implications of carrying the cost of these shortfalls forward as part of stock are exactly the same as for any other type of overhead.

Overhead allocations is clearly a potential tool for the creative accountant. However, it can also be a most constructive management tool when properly applied. The process of identifying the particular costs associated with a product can have significant benefits for the company. One of the country's leading retailers has found that by identifying the real costs of different product lines it can assess profitability much more effectively. Overhead allocation suddenly becomes a creative management tool.

By way of a simple illustration consider the following. A company sells equal amounts of the two products which retail at the same selling price. Product A is three times bigger than Product B. If the costs are allocated to each product in line with the underlying reality the following analysis emerges:

	Total	Product A	Product B
Sales	220	110	110
Less cost of sales	100	50	50
Gross profit	120	60	60
Less operating costs			
Warehousing	40	30	10
Delivery	20	15	5
Retail outlet	20	15	5
Operating profit	40	–	40
Less central costs	10	5	5
Net profit (loss)	30	(5)	35

Suddenly the picture is transformed. Two products which had exactly the same gross margins produce very different results once all costs are allocated. The process can be quite subjective but more sophisticated technology means that the exercise can be undertaken with much greater accuracy than used to be the case. Properly managed it can deliver some quite exciting results.

So far the discussion of stock has centred on the cost which should be attributed to it for year end valuation purposes. However, you will remember that the basic accounting rule is that stock should be reported in the accounts at the lower of cost or net realizable value. The implication of this is that where stock is worth less than what it cost to buy or produce then it should be valued at what it could be sold off for, if anything. This basis will be appropriate for those items which have been damaged and have become obsolete or, because of their slow-moving nature, might have to be sold at a knock-down price.

Once again the decision on whether an item's value has fallen below its cost is arbitrary in nature and therefore requires the subjectivity which is the lifeblood of the creative accountant. It has to be pointed out that in some situations the write-down of an item of stock to below its cost cannot be avoided, particularly when it is a question of physical deterioration or damage. In these cases it would not only be breaking the accounting rules to avoid the write-off but also constitutes imprudent management.

However, when the decision has to be taken on the grounds of obsolescence or because items are slow moving then there is much more flexibility. Again though, failure to recognize that some parts of the inventory have fallen in value below their original cost may result in longer-term difficulties. Where this has happened the fact must be accounted for at some stage and perhaps the best that can be done is for the provision to be deferred to a later period.

One way round the problem of ugly blemishes in the shape of large write-downs is to make a regular provision for obsolete, damaged and slow-moving stocks. The disadvantage of this is that while it represents an annual charge to profits, it does have the distinct plus point of bringing an element of consistency to the proceedings. The level of the annual provision can be established by reference to a particular formula. It may simply be a percentage of the total year end value of the stock or it could be calculated on some other appropriate basis.

The provision can also be used as a very effective smoothing tool. By making overly prudent provisions in years of plenty a company then has the flexibility either to do away with the write-down provision in the years of famine or, in the very lean years, actually write some of the provision back to help boost year end stock. However, using an annual provision method of accounting for stock obsolescence does not excuse a company from maintaining a close watch over the actual state of the inventory. If a regular and realistic assessment of the stock is not made then it can lead to the provision getting totally out of line. This is contrary to the general objective of avoiding fluctuations. The company will want to avoid making any unusual write-downs or write-backs which will only serve to attract the stock market's attention. It won't go down too well with the auditors either, since they will have been happily approving the level of provisions which had been made in previous years. Consistency is fine and commendable until a company realizes that it has been consistently wrong and that embarrassing adjustments are called for.

Any business which is involved in large purchases of raw materials which are dependent on the commodity or other independently fluctuating markets for their price will have to pay particular attention to the net realizable value question. Some inopportune purchasing policies or sudden decline in the open market price of a particular commodity can cause problems. Generally it should be possible to avoid having to make significant provisions to reflect the vagaries of the market-place but a permanent decline in prices or plain old inefficient purchasing may require write-downs and it is

66

important for the company, therefore, to be well aware of the movements in commodity prices so that the year end approach to the stock valuation can be tailored to mask these unfortunate and perhaps unusual circumstances.

For companies where the level of the stocks does not perhaps justify an annual provision the approach to write-offs will be tempered by the stock position in a particular year. Once again the objective must be to maintain a realistic value for stock but to do so in a way which does not result in wild fluctuations. This means that a careful balancing exercise might have to be carried out, which is designed on the one hand to boost the stock valuation in preparation for reducing it again with the other in the shape of a write-down. There may well be a case for deferring some provisions until the next accounting period if to take all the appropriate write-offs in the same year would bring a sharp reduction in the stock valuation. All the time the creative accountant will be fully aware of the importance of maintaining a steady progression in the company's stock profits.

Stock is not only important for the purposes of smoothing a company's reported profitability. It can also be put to use quite profitably in the context of transfer pricing where goods are being produced for onward sale to another division or an overseas subsidiary. There can be very good reasons for wanting to manipulate the cost at which these intra-group goods are sold. Normally this will be to minimize tax bills. The objective will be to maximize costs in a high tax area and minimize them in a lower tax country. The allocation of overheads can become quite critical in determining the overall profitability of individual divisions.

This tax avoidance may be regarded as an admirable objective by many. However, it is one which is fraught with danger. Smoothing profits to present a more realistic picture of a company's profits profile is one thing. Fiddling the taxman is another. Those who are inclined to minimize their tax bill should exercise extreme caution.

Whatever the motives for tinkering with this crucial area of the accounts it should be borne in mind that all the work of the creative accountant is rendered useless if the company does not have an effective and efficient control over its stock and its stocktaking procedures. If the physical stock is already being tampered with lower down in the organization then the chances of senior management retaining a firm grip on its own manipulation measures are much reduced. It has to be remembered that for many businesses, its stock is in a readily realizable condition and is therefore something of a target for light-fingered employees. There are many examples of fraud in varying degrees of size and complexity which have been linked directly with the company's stock and the management's failure to maintain adequate control over it.

One example of a highly effective fraud involving the theft of stock came from a building supplies company which had a number of branches spread around the country each controlled by a manager who had responsibility for stock-taking procedures at his branch. At one of the biggest branches a junior manager who had a taste for fast women and slow horses decided that the only way to keep himself in the style to which his girlfriends and bookmaker had become accustomed was to indulge in a little private enterprise. In effect he set up his own small business which unfortunately relied entirely on his employer's stock for its existence. Without wishing to cast a slur on the building industry in general there are some elements of it which would look more at home firing six-shooters in the air, sporting ten-gallon hats and chasing after a posse of Sioux Indians.

It was these cowboys who provided the customer base for the enterprising junior manager. Nods and winks were exchanged for fistfuls of used fivers and the company's stock quietly found its way out of the warehouse and into the back of Ford Transit vans of dubious roadworthiness and even more dubious ownership. However, the fraudster was well aware of the implications of his dirty deeds. It was he who effectively ran the branch accounts since the senior manager had little interest in this rather mundane and boring task. He was also largely responsible for overseeing the annual stocktaking and realized that the missing stock would be detected when the branch's gross profit margin was analysed. He therefore maintained very careful records of the stock which left by the back door under the cover of darkness.

To compensate for the stolen stock he then placed empty boxes, which would previously have contained high value items, around the warehouse in the most awkward of places. Had the boxes been full their value would have equated roughly to that of the absentee items. At the time of the annual stocktaking, which always took place on New Year's Eve with opening time beckoning, the junior manager made sure that nobody got too close to the empty boxes and they were duly counted on the assumption that they were full. The fraud worked perfectly year in year out. The gross margins were maintained and everybody was happy. However, the branch's business eventually outgrew the size of the warehouse and a bigger and better home was found for it.

It was at this stage that the junior manager came well and truly unstuck. The move into the new home was planned for New Year's Eve so that it would coincide with the stocktaking thus allowing two birds, and as it transpired a thief, to be killed with one stone. The size of the move and the company's pride in its new bigger branch resulted in a swarm of head office staff coming down to help out with the task. The poor junior manager looked on aghast as eager pasty-faced clerks from the accounts department gleefully and innocently crumpled up the occasional empty box with the enthusiasm often found in those who only have to undertake manual work for the one day. As the day wore on the mound of flattened cardboard boxes grew higher, still without attracting too much attention. It was only when the stocktaking was completed and the valuation carried out that the full significance of the empty boxes and the enormity of the crime became apparent. A gross margin which had been steadily maintained at around 20 per cent crumbled to a little over 6 per cent when an accurate closing stock figure was used in the calculation for the first time in some years.

The junior manager had no choice but to come clean. He did not quite break down in tears wailing 'it's a fair cop but society is to blame' but he was sufficiently penitent and the company's embarrassment was sufficiently great for him to get away with little more than instant dismissal. It is a cautionary tale for all companies. They should always be aware that their innocent manipulation of stock at head office might be being imitated and undermined by some altogether more sinister manipulation elsewhere in the organization.

It is not just fraudsters who threaten to destroy the company's carefully planned pattern of smooth growth. Inefficient managers who are conscious that they are not meeting performance targets might also be tempted to indulge in a little creative accounting of their own. The sensitive nature of stock and the ease with which it can be manipulated makes it an obvious target for artificial adjustment which will make a poor financial performance, well below budget, become much more palatable. The difficulty is that while all appears to be going well and targets seem to be being met quite comfortably there is a danger that the senior management will leave the individual branch or subsidiary to its own devices with only minimum supervision. However, the number of provisions which appear in company accounts relating to 'stock write-downs at a subsidiary' suggest that the hands-off approach to management is not always appropriate. The senior management must therefore be prepared to relinquish their role as creative accounting poachers and occasionally take on the unfamiliar mantle of gamekeeper.

If effective control over the individual company and branch assets is maintained then the task of implementing smoothing measures at the group level is made that much easier. The opportunities for creativity in the area of stock and work in progress is just too good to be ruined by slip-ups elsewhere. It is another variation on the theme of looking after the pennies and letting the pounds look after themselves. But stock is not only an area of great scope for manipulation. It is also an area where the chances of the outside world finding out exactly what you have been up to are remote to say the least.

This becomes apparent from a cursory glance at the ways in which companies disclose their accounting policy on stocks and work in progress. The accounts of English China Clays for the year ended 31 December 1993 state quite simply that 'Stocks are valued at the lower of the cost and estimated net realizable value. For work in progress and finished goods manufactured by the group, cost includes, where appropriate, an element of overhead cost.'

This policy is not untypical but hardly allows the user the opportunity to gauge with any accuracy how stock has been valued. What it does do, however, is confirm just how much subjective judgement will be used. Net realizable value is estimated and only an element of overhead cost is included where appropriate.

The absence of information may not be intentional but there is no doubt that it does no harm to a company if it gives away as little as possible on its stock valuation policy and retains a shroud of uncertainty behind which it can make the necessary refinements to the approach adopted as and when required. There is no overt pressure on companies to improve this aspect of their financial accounts and in its absence few companies will go out of their way to make improvements voluntarily.

It is a sad fact that few shareholders pay too much attention anyway to a company's accounting policies. This is regrettable since this is the closest that the company ever comes to revealing how it has arrived at the figures which are contained in the accounts. Perhaps a greater interest from shareholders might provoke an improvement in the standard of accounting policy disclosure from the companies they own. Many accounting policies are couched in such vague and often garbled terms that they probably restrict rather than improve any understanding of the business. However, while the companies and their shareholders happily co-habit in a world of mutual uninterest in accounting policies there is little prospect of an improvement.

Perhaps if shareholders were aware of the kind of accounting tricks which are carried out in arriving at the stock valuation, then they might be encouraged to take more than their current passing interest in the underlying policies.

6. Current Assets

A company's debtors and creditors tend to be rather overshadowed by their more illustrious neighbours of stock and cash or borrowings in the current assets area of the balance sheet. The lack of attention which is paid to them is misplaced if not misguided since debtor and creditor management can be an important influence in determining a company's cash flow position. It follows that the quicker that debts are collected and the slower that creditors are paid, the better. This frees funds which would otherwise have been financing working capital requirements for use elsewhere in the business. However, moderation, as with all things, is called for. This overzealous approach to working capital management could, if not carefully controlled, result in a disproportionate amount of current liability arising. If the company's resources are tied up in long-term and fixed assets then it may face problems in meeting the short-term liabilities as they fall due.

There are creative accounting opportunities within current assets and liabilities but they also provide a useful analytical tool for accounts users. A careful analysis of the relationship between creditors and debtors can give an important indication of the company's performance and prospects. A fairly even match between the two is normally quite acceptable although this must also be set against the level of the company's other current assets. Similarly, an examination of the relationship between the debtors and creditors and the sales and purchases which gave rise to them can be equally informative. If turnover is falling then the level of debtors would be expected to follow suit and a failure for it so to do might be an indication of some kind of problem with the collection procedures.

Although a detailed examination of debtors and creditors is perhaps not a regular feature of the City's assessment of a company's performance and prospects this does not mean that these current assets and liabilities can be left to their own devices. Once again any unusual fluctuations in the figures will be picked up and used as evidence against the company so it is still important to ensure that the relevant figures proceed in a quiet and orderly fashion. The converse of this is that both debtors and creditors can be used in a positive fashion to help achieve this objective.

The most obvious area for attention is the ominous-sounding subject of bad debts. As a rule these are things to be avoided. Careful credit control and vetting of new customers can help mitigate the circumstances where bad debts might arise but it is a sad fact of commercial life that some businesses simply cannot pay their way and go to the wall leaving their creditors high and dry and facing an unwelcome bad debt provision.

It therefore becomes important for a company to take a realistic attitude to the problem and plan ahead for the inevitable debts which will occur. That planning comes in the shape of providing for bad debts in the most constructive fashion. Often the best approach will be to make a general provision on an annual basis. This is not dissimilar to the concept of making an annual provision for obsolescent stock. Again it has the advantage of bringing an element of consistency to the situation which will offset the discomfort of the charge which has to be made to the profit and loss account.

The general bad debt provision may simply be calculated as a consistent proportion of the total debtors. On the other hand it may be linked to the age of debtors. The longer the debt has been outstanding the less chance there is of its being recovered and thus the greater the chance of its requiring a subsequent provision. The company may therefore provide against all debts over a certain age and then make provisions against the younger debts on a reducing scale of proportions. A prudent approach to bad debt provisions at an early stage will reduce the chances of a company being taken by surprise later should a large debt suddenly go bad. Even if such a specific bad debt had not been provided against there might be no need to incur an ugly write-off scar since this can be set against the general provision which had already been created. The provision will then require some topping up in subsequent years but this can be done in a more leisurely and less obtrusive fashion.

The same general provision can also be used as an accounting tool for assisting with the profits smoothing process. The provision is gradually built up while profits growth is good. When those increases slow down or even go into decline then the company will be able to reduce the impact of this change in fortunes by either halting any further additions to the bad debt provision or in some cases actually releasing a part of the provision and writing it back as a contributor to profit for the year on the grounds that it is no longer necessary. This affords a very useful element of control over the reported profits which is perhaps not in itself sufficient to combat any major change in fortunes but can certainly help to remove some of the smaller unwanted fluctuations.

The opportunities for inflating debtors are somewhat limited although a company can perhaps make some attempt to do so by its approach on trade debtors. These are normally offered as an incentive for debtors to pay their invoices promptly and will take the form of a reduction in the cash which is due on settlement. The sooner the customer pays the greater the discount. Normally a company will include the gross amount of the invoice value as part of sales for the year. Any discounts which are claimed will be treated as marketing or administrative costs and charged as an expense rather than as a reduction of sales value. A company might therefore be tempted to adopt a similar approach to the year end debtors which will include the gross amounts outstanding. The problem with this is that it can then be argued that the debts are being stated at more than their net realizable value which conflicts with company law. In this position the company will be forced to make some provision for those discounts. This of course is an arbitrary decision which will be only loosely based on the past take-up of discounts.

There might also be an added element of flexibility in the way that the provision for the discounts is disclosed. The company could well argue that it has the right to choose to report the provision in the accounts either as a reduction of total debtors or as an addition to its creditors. Normally the set-off between assets and liabilities is forbidden but this does not affect the situation relating to discounts. In fact the company might well struggle to try to justify not setting the provision against debtors since these would still be disclosed at an amount greater than their net realizable value. It is worth a try, though.

One further way which might be considered as a means of pushing up the figure reported in the accounts as debtors is to boost the level of prepayments. These relate to expenses which have been settled in one accounting period but which relate in part to a subsequent year. Telephone bills, for instance, always charge the rental of the equipment one quarter in advance. Rates are also normally paid in advance and unless the rateable year coincides with the company's own accounting period then there will be some element of prepayment. Any such amounts will be excluded from the charge to profits for the year and treated as an asset of the company. The prepayments can be disclosed either as a separate category in the balance sheet or as part of debtors.

So if a company wants some reason to boost its total debtors, perhaps to offset the impact of some unusually high bad debt provision, then it might well resort to prepayments as the means of accomplishing this. There are two difficulties with this. First the bringing forward of the payment will result in a reduction in cash although this may actually be part of the strategy. The second problem is that it is often hard to find items which can be categorized as prepayments. There is a limit to the number of phone bills and rate demands which can be settled ahead of the year end. However, if the company leases some or all of its buildings then it may be possible to make some substantial prepayments of rentals for the forthcoming year. However, the desire for creative accounting must be tempered by the commercial viability of the decision. The prepayment is going to result in a reduction of income which might have been earned on the cash and this must be taken into account.

This artificial increase in debtors is only reflected in the main balance sheet. The observant reader of the accounts will discover what the company has done if he refers to the notes to the accounts and the cash flow statement. The analysis of the total debtors figure which must be provided has to disclose as a separate item the amount of any prepayments. This disclosure requirement perhaps reduces the effectiveness of the tactic although the company can still gamble on shareholders and other interested parties failing to delve as deep as the notes to the accounts.

One further point relating to debtors is their value as a form of funding. Debts are an asset of the business and as such represent an opportunity to secure funds. In the US discounting receivables facilities, as they are known, are often used to help companies improve their cash position. This is in fact a form of off-balance-sheet finance which is covered in more detail elsewhere. It allows a company artificially to reduce its debt position. The funds provided by the facility are secured against a company's trade debtors. This boosts the company's overall debt position but the cost of the facility is disguised in that it will be treated as fees rather than interest. In the UK the factoring of debts, where essentially the amount owing by customers is sold to a third party in return for a cash payment, is commonplace. In terms of flattering the overall debt position of the company it is quite effective.

Scope for manipulation of a company's working capital is not, of course, restricted to debtors. Creditors have their fair share to contribute to the creative accountant's armoury.

Given that creditors are almost the mirror image of debtors it will come as no surprise to discover that many of the techniques which can be used to improve the superficial impression of a set of accounts are the exact opposite of those which can be used when dealing with amounts which are owed by customers.

Take trade discounts for instance. While it is the company which is offering these to debtors there is an incentive to account for the gross amount of the invoice. However, once the boot is switched to the other foot and it is the company itself which is in a position to claim discounts through prompt payment then there will be a tendency to treat invoices from suppliers on a net basis after deducting the discount receivable. This has the immediate effect of reducing the cost of sales and at the same time reducing the amount which is disclosed in the balance sheet as trade creditors.

The same role reversal is encountered when dealing with the converse of prepayments which are known as accruals. The purpose of these is to take account of the cost of goods or services which the company has had the benefit of but for which it has not yet been invoiced. These may take the form of goods delivered towards the end of the year which the supplier has not got round to invoicing. Another example is that old faithful the telephone bill. For while the equipment rental is charged in advance, the actual calls made are billed in arrears. Thus a company is obliged to accrue for the cost of those calls which were made before the year end but which had not been invoiced at that date.

On a more serious level companies can also use provisions to counter the impact of a quite adverse reversal of their operating fortunes. This was most appreciated by some advertising agencies which have made provisions for the rent on surplus office space. During the glory days of the eighties the advertising industry boomed and as companies expanded their empires they snapped up office accommodation which of course had to be in keeping with the glamorous and expansive image it was felt appropriate to have. The global recession of the early nineties brought them down to earth with a bump. Contraction and survival became the driving imperatives and as jobs were shed and businesses closed down some agencies found themselves with more office space than they needed. It was office space which had been let at quite fancy rents. Unfortunately it was office space that no one else particularly wanted.

The rent still had to be paid, which was a drain on cash and also on profits. The solution came through a provision for the cost of the rental on this surplus space. It can be argued that this was merely a prudent approach to the problem but the effect was quite intriguing. Although it resulted in a one-off charge this was entirely acceptable in the context of a business which was undergoing significant restructuring in order to survive. More importantly it protected the longer-term profit and loss account from the cost of that surplus office space. It did nothing to halt the drain on cash flow, the rental after all still had to be paid, but it did allow an agency to inflate profits artificially once the one-off hit had been taken.

The converse of this is not to make any provision at all and simply charge the rental against profits as they fall due. However, this whole area has been dogged by uncertainty. The Urgent Issues Task Force in its draft abstract on the subject supported entirely the approach which the advertising agencies had been using for some time.

The UITF concluded initially that when a property substantially ceases to be used for the purposes of the business or a commitment is entered into which would cause this to occur, provision should be made to the extent that the recoverable amount of the interest in the property is expected to be insufficient to cover the future obligations relating to the lease. The provision should be based on market conditions at the balance sheet date taking account of what is likely to happen in practice. The provision should also take account of other on-going expenses such as rates and security together with any costs associated with vacating the property.

However, three months after the draft was published it was then withdrawn after arguments that the rules could discourage companies from taking out long leases. We are therefore left with the unusual situation where in essence the UITF has condoned one form of creative accounting and then backed down. The area remains even greyer than before with the rules now so flexible that companies can argue with great authority that a provision should or should not be made.

Quantifying a provision for office rents is as easy or as difficult as a company wants the exercise to be. When dealing with provisions and accruals generally there is clearly a significant element of subjective judgement involved in assessing what level of accruals ought to be made. Often that subjectivity is removed by the arrival of an invoice shortly after the year end and before the accounts are finalized. However, there will be times when the company has to use little more than guesswork when deciding what accruals to make. Assuming that the approach adopted is not outrageous it should be possible for the management to make some gentle understatement of the true amount. The effect of understating the accruals is to reduce the liability which has to be disclosed in the balance sheet and at the same time reduces the expenses which are charged to the profit and loss account in the year. It should be stressed that consistent material understatement of such liabilities is getting very close to the bone which is marked fraud. This of course is against the principle of creative accounting which relies for its success and credibility on strict compliance with the law.

The line between creative accounting and fraud can sometimes be very thin and very frail. The line sometimes disappears from view altogether when the question of recognizing liabilities is addressed. The basic rule which runs throughout the standards laid down by the accountancy profession is that all losses should be recognized and provided for as soon as their existence is discovered while profits should only be accounted for when they are realized. It is a rule, however, which is often broken. There is a distinct reluctance among companies to take account of some liabilities which are looming on the horizon. The uncertainty which often surrounds these items makes it easier for a company to dismiss them particularly when the potential liability would not crystallize until some time in the future.

The possible cost of legal actions a company faces, for instance, is very rarely recognized. There is a very good reason for this in that a company is not prepared to admit any degree of liability when a legal action has been started. The fact that a provision has been made in the accounts could be interpreted by the other side as some kind of admission of guilt. Very often there are also good legal grounds for not making any provision. However, once an action moves closer to court the arguments for making a provision become stronger. No matter what the lawyers say there is no guarantee that a case will be won in court. There are also some accounting arguments for making a discrete provision. If the company loses then it has already taken the pain of the financial loss. If it wins, however, the provision can be written back as a useful boost to profits.

Of course, legal actions are not the only type of liability which may arise. However, the principles of recognition are very similar although less constrained since the legal implications will not feature as largely in the equation. The underlying considerations, though, are essentially unchanged and the decision on the provision will be dependent on the company's current trading and projected profits profile.

It would be misleading to suggest that liabilities are just nasty things which have to be avoided wherever possible. There are positive creative accounting points which should not be overlooked. These are exactly the same as those which apply to the assessment of bad debt provisions. By setting up a liability, perhaps for warranty agreements on the company's products, the business is able to maintain stability within the reported results and avoid any nasty shocks to the system which could threaten to ruin the smoothing process.

The management should also not overlook the benefits of a taking-it-on-the-chin approach to liabilities and provisions. This is discussed in more detail in the chapter on the profit and loss account. In summary though a company sets up a provision when it is most convenient. This could be when profitability is very strong. It could be when big exceptional write-offs are being made.

Once those provisions are set up they are then carried forward in the balance sheet and the actual costs are written off to them as and when they are incurred thus leaving the company's trading performance unscathed.

There is some uncertainty and confusion over how such provisions should be disclosed in the accounts. It is clearly in the company's interests to give as little away as possible about them if they are being used as part of the smoothing process or if they relate to some contended legal action. However, the Companies Acts have anticipated these liabilities and there is a requirement for 'provisions for liabilities and charges' to be disclosed as a separate item in the balance sheet with a more detailed analysis being presented by way of a note to the accounts. The 1985 Act also goes as far as providing a definition of these items describing them as 'Any amount retained as reasonably necessary for the purpose of providing for any liability or loss which is either likely to be incurred or certain to be incurred but uncertain as to the amount or as to the date on which it will arise.'

The law is quite precise on this point and it is difficult to argue that these provisions should be disclosed as part of the trade creditors figure or as an accrual. There may be some cases where such arguments can be presented and accepted and some companies will always make an effort to argue for the less explicit disclosure. In most cases the company must reveal, for each provision, the aggregate amount at the beginning and end of the year, any amounts which have been transferred to or from the provision during the financial year and, more importantly, the source and application of those transfers.

On the surface this might appear to blow any chance of a company keeping secret the purposes of and movements on a specific provision. However, there is an escape route from this baring-all scenario. It comes in the shape of that dreadful five-lettered word 'other'. No doubt when the word was first invented, perhaps in some Stone-Age Scrabble game, its creator did not realize what a favour he was doing for the creative accountants who, centuries later, would be acting out their own version of rubbing two stones together aided and abetted by that random selection of five letters which were thrown so conveniently together.

For although the Companies Act says that an analysis must be provided for each provision, it has no objection, it seems, to a collective category of 'other provisions'. It is within this category that a company will be able to hide its more sensitive provisions although it will then become more difficult to disguise the ways in which it has used these as a profits smoothing mechanism. The best way around this problem is for the company to hide any write-backs to the profit and loss account in among the amount disclosed, in the analysis in the notes to the accounts, as being utilized in the year. This is probably more effective than netting the write-backs against any charges to the profit and loss account. It should be pointed out, though, that while the 'other provisions' escape route should be available to cope with most situations, the law insists that any individual provision contained therein which is itself material, should be disclosed separately. The decision on whether or not an item is material is of course arbitrary and therefore a company will usually be able to retain anonymity.

So although the overall disclosure requirements make the creative accountant's job that little bit harder, there is still sufficient flexibility within the rules on both creditors and debtors to allow some gentle massaging of the figures. It has to be remembered that the disclosure rules apply only to the company's published accounts which appear some weeks after the preliminary announcement of profits for the year. Given that it is this announcement which is going to attract the share price and be examined by City analysts then the manipulation should still achieve the desired effect even though it might be later uncovered by a closer review of the annual accounts.

This says more about the workings of the City than it does about the relevance of company accounts but it emphasizes the importance for shareholders and potential investors to scrutinize the published financial statements when they finally appear. A careful examination of the detailed notes on both debtors and creditors should give at least a broad indication of how the company has used these areas to play around with its reported profit. The accounts have to provide a better basis for taking a considered view of the company's prospects than an often sparse preliminary announcement.

7. Share Capital

As the chapters on off-balance-sheet finance and borrowings demonstrate there is a clear demand among companies to treat the long-term funding of the business as equity rather than debt. If those funds can be treated as capital rather than borrowings then it has quite positive implications for the gearing ratio of the company.

However, while so much attention is focused on the classification question very little attention is paid to the opportunities for creative accounting which lie within a company's own share capital. For many businesses the only interest in its shares stems from the price at which they are quoted on the stock exchange. They are simply things which can be issued to raise more money and used to finance acquisitions. The only interesting aspect of the company's shares is that their price on the stock market never reflects the company's past performance and future prospects adequately.

However, this preoccupation with the quoted price and its movements tends to prevent a company's management from picking up on the scope which now exists for taking a more active interest in its own capital. That scope is provided by the provisions of company legislation which make it possible for a business to buy its own shares. The opportunity to use this tactic has often been overlooked by companies although there are some notable exceptions.

There has, for instance, been a relatively high degree of buy-back activity among some of the privatized electricity companies. Blessed with strong cash flows and given the nature of the business they have found the buy-back programme a quite fruitful means of distributing that cash back into the stock market.

The privatized utilities, however, are uniquely placed and buy-back programmes are less widely used in other sectors. Where schemes have been arranged or even hinted at the stock market reaction has tended to be favourable although there is no guarantee that this will always be the case. The uncertainty of market reaction and management's own wariness of this approach still make the buy-back more of an option than a necessity.

The decision by a company on whether to buy in its own shares will depend on a number of factors. The relationship between net asset value and the share price in the market will be important. So, too, will be the company's own cash resources and the demands for those resources elsewhere in the group. The likely reception by the stock market of the move will also be a factor. For the company which does buy in its own shares the advantages can be significant.

Take two companies of equal size and similar activity. Both have 10 million shares in issue and a share price of £5 which gives them both a market capitalization of £50 million. The net assets of both companies are equivalent to £7 a share which values both companies on this basis at £70 million. Both companies earn profits attributable to shareholders of £18 million. Company A decides that it will purchase 10 per cent of its own shares and obtain its shareholders' approval to do so. Company B refrains from taking a similar step. The effect of the different approaches is as follows:

	Company A	Company B
Shares in issue	9m	10m
Price per share	£5	£5
Market capitalization	£45m	£50m
Net assets per share	£7.22	£7
Net assets value	£65m	£70m
Earnings per share	£1.94	£1.80

The illustration is based on the assumption that the purchase of Company A's own shares is made out of its own cash resources. The loss of interest on that cash is estimated to reduce attributable profits by £500,000 in the year under review.

Even after allowing for this adjustment it is clear that Company A's financial position appears to look much more attractive than that of Company B. It increases not just the value of net assets per share but as part of the same transaction also increases the earnings attributable to each share.

The stock market implications of the share purchase should be to push Company A's share price higher. Its stock will now appear to be much cheaper than that of Company B. First, it has a lower price earnings ratio which implies that the shares should increase in value to reflect this. Second, Company A's shares are now at an even greater discount to net assets than they were before, which should also encourage a greater upward momentum in the price. It may also be that the very action of a big purchase of shares may prompt the market to mark the shares up simply as a reaction to the activity.

That reaction, however, will depend very much on how the market interprets the share buy-in. It may be seen as an indication that the company's management is sharp and well aware that the shares were undervalued and has thus acted sensibly in the best interest of the shareholders by securing the stock at a substantial discount to net assets. The stock market may, in these circumstances, see the transaction as something of a bull point and mark the shares up in recognition of this.

However, there is no guarantee that this is the reaction which will greet the buy-in. Bearing in mind that once these shares have been purchased by the company, it is obliged to cancel them, then the stock market may regard the action as rather futile and somewhat negative. The City might ask, with some justification, why is this company having to resort to such tactics? Could it not employ the funds used to finance the share purchase in a more constructive and perhaps more positive way?

When a company is sitting on a big pile of cash the market is always keen to discover what plans it has for spending it. Hopes that it may be used to finance a take-over are built up, but if all the company does is buy its own shares then these may come tumbling down. The market may begin to believe that the management is short of ideas on how to spend the cash. Might it not be better spent on developing the business? The likelihood of getting a positive reaction to the purchase of the company's own shares will be reduced if money has to be borrowed to finance the transaction. The dividend payments which are forgone will not be sufficient to offset the increased interest payments which will be incurred and these in turn will restrict the group's cash flow. The market might also interpret the purchase as a desperate attempt to try to support a share price which has been showing signs of weakness.

It is not just share price considerations which will influence the company's decision on whether or not to go into the market to buy in its own shares. Such an action will also reflect the company's perceptions of the other commercial factors which affect its long-term future and, in some cases, its long-term independence.

For instance if the management believes that there is an unwelcome predator waiting in the wings to launch a take-over bid then it may well be prudent to move in and buy up any loose shares which are floating around on the market. This reduces the opportunities for the predator to pick up those shares itself and use them as a platform to launch the bid. However, such an action may also present some longer-term problems for the company to proceed with its own business development strategy, particularly if this involves an element of acquisition. Not only does the share buy-in wear down the company's liquid resources or stretch its borrowings capabilities but it also might suggest an element of inconsistency in the management philosophy. If the company goes into the market and buys its own shares and then a few months later issues more shares in order to finance an acquisition then eyebrows will be raised.

However, these apparently bearish points should not deter a company from at least examining the possibility of buying its own shares. There is certainly no harm in looking and indeed no charge for so doing. It has already been demonstrated that the company's share price can benefit considerably from such a move and this in itself is a sufficient incentive to review the situation. It may well be that the stock market price of the shares so undervalues the company that buying them in is simply too attractive a proposition to miss. There is certainly no harm in preparing the ground which will allow the purchase to be made and it should be a standard policy for a company to have secured, as a matter of course, the necessary approval from shareholders to implement such a programme of action.

It is therefore essential that the company's management is well aware of the legal and other requirements which govern the purchase of its own shares. The 1985 Companies Act lays down several rules which must be adhered to. The power for a company to purchase its own shares must be embodied in its articles of association and the incorporation of such power in those articles must be approved by the shareholders. The company must also seek approval from shareholders to proceed with a purchase of its own shares. For transactions which will be performed outside a recognized stock exchange a special resolution must be passed. Transactions which will be carried out on a recognized stock exchange need only the approval of an ordinary resolution. Such an ordinary resolution must specify the number of shares to be acquired and the maximum and minimum price which will be paid. The authority which the shareholders give to the management by way of passing this resolution lasts for a maximum of eighteen months from the date of the resolution being passed. The expiry date must be specified after which further approval from shareholders must be sought.

The resolution should be drafted in such a way that the company retains a high degree of flexibility over the number of shares which it can purchase and at what price, but at the same time is in no way committed to make a purchase if market conditions make it an unrealistic proposition. Companies which are considering a share buy-in would be well advised to seek authority from their shareholders even if the prospects of a buy-in are remote. Forward planning at an early stage relieves the company of the embarrassment of having to seek a rushed approval from shareholders at a later date which in itself could arouse the stock market's suspicions.

GEC provides in its 1994 accounts a good insight into the ground which needs to be covered in a resolution which would be put to the meeting. A section in the directors' report dealing with the authority for the company to purchase its own shares reads:

At the last Annual General Meeting shareholders renewed and extended the Company's previous authority to enable it to make market purchases on the London Stock Exchange of up to an aggregate of 400 million ordinary shares of 5p each being approximately 14.7 per cent of the Company's issued share capital, at not more than 400p and not less than 5p per share until 2 March 1995.

Under previous authorities the Company purchased 79,604,067 of its shares in the two years ended 31 March 1986 representing approximately 3 per cent of the Company's issued share capital; no further purchases have been made during the eight years ended 31 March 1994.

The directors consider that further purchases by the company of its ordinary shares for cancellation may in certain circumstances be advantageous to shareholders through resultant increased earnings per share. They believe that the existing authority should be renewed and extended for a maximum period of eighteen months from the date of the forthcoming Annual General Meeting. This would be on the basis that the maximum price for shares purchased in the market shall not exceed the lesser of 400p, and in accordance with the London Stock Exchange requirements an amount equal to 5 per cent above the average of the middle market quotations taken from the London Stock Exchange Daily Official List for the ten business days before the purchase is made. The minimum price per share shall be not less than 5p, being the par value of the share. Accordingly Resolution Number 13 in the Notice of Meeting will be proposed at the forthcoming Annual General Meeting.

The 1985 Companies Act also specifies that only fully paid shares can be repurchased. These must then be cancelled which in turn reduces the issued share capital. The purchase consideration for the shares bought in must be financed out of the company's profits which are available for distribution. If the shares had been issued at a premium then that premium on a repurchase does not have to be paid for out of distributable profits but can be offset against the appropriate element of the relevant share premium account providing the aggregate amount of nominal capital and distributable reserves is maintained.

For shares which are repurchased entirely out of distributable profits, then an amount equal to the nominal value of those shares must be transferred to a capital redemption reserve. This ensures that the company's capital is maintained. Finally, the Act specifies that the purchase price must be paid on completion of the transaction.

These provisions may appear to be quite complicated but they are little more than paper adjustments and do nothing to detract from the clear benefits which can arise through buying-in the shares. However, the rules on share repurchases are not restricted to those laid down by company law. The Stock Exchange has also seen fit to weigh in with its own requirements which while providing additional factors to be considered by the company are in fact less technical in nature and more related to the practical aspects of these types of transaction.

The rules only apply to listed companies and state that in any twelve-month period a company can only make purchases of up to 15 per cent of its own capital. If the company wants to exceed this figure then it can only do so by way of a partial offer or tender offer. The Stock Exchange also insists that a company cannot buy its own shares in the two months which precede the announcement of its annual or half-year results. Neither of these restrictions is particularly onerous. It is unlikely that a company would want to buy in more than 15 per cent of its capital in any twelve-month period. Similarly, the rule forbidding repurchases in four months of the year still allows sufficient flexibility of timing to ensure that the company can take advantage of market conditions as and when they are suited to a share buy-in.

A further consideration is the tax implications of share repurchases which can affect their viability. Both the company's own position and that of the vendors must be examined quite closely to ensure that the transaction is carried out in the most efficient way.

Again, these considerations should not act as a deterrent although they may be critical in determining whether the time is right to indulge in a share buy-in. Judging by the lack of activity on the share repurchasing front, perhaps it is fair to assume that companies have been put off by the various restrictions. However, by giving up so easily many businesses are missing out on a readily available creative accounting tool which, unlike many others, does not rely on a literal interpretation of the relevant rules but is actually encouraged by them. Certainly it is not a tool which can be used too often and any abuse will devalue the benefits which might otherwise have been available. However, a prudent and considered use of share buy-ins can produce a considerable advantage for the company and indeed its own shareholders.

8. Fixed Assets

The great thing about fixed assets is that their values are completely mobile. For many companies these assets are the backbone of the business, providing the foundation and framework which allows it to carry out its operations. Yet despite their importance, the rules which govern the reported values of fixed assets are remarkably flexible.

That flexibility is the more remarkable given the starting point for the valuation process. This will, in the large majority of cases, be the cost of the asset which is rarely open to manipulation. Be it a company car or piece of land, the purchase price will set the benchmark from which the creative accounting process begins. There is little scope for tampering with original cost but after that there is unlimited scope for making fixed assets work for the business in every sense of the phrase. That scope is more pronounced because the value placed on the assets can be adjusted either upwards or downwards almost at will.

The justification for this creativity is actually embodied in company law which permits three different bases for valuations of fixed assets to be adopted. Alongside the old favourite of historical cost which is simply the price paid for an asset, the legislation also allows market valuations to be used. Companies can also state their fixed assets at current cost although the law gives no indication of what it means by this rather vague term. Given this overt approval of a variety of valuation methods it is not surprising that most businesses are more than happy to take advantage of them.

This array of choices is offered in recognition of the corporate sector's desire to reflect more fairly the value of its assets to the respective businesses. It is not an unreasonable proposition. However, the decision on what basis or combination of bases to use rests solely with the company thereby opening the way for a great amount of creativity which becomes inevitable when subjective judgements are called for in large quantities.

That subjectivity and the dilemmas it can cause is illustrated by the approach that British Airways has taken on its fleet of Concordes. Supersonic and sleek the jet may be but it is valued at nothing in the airline's accounts. The decision to write the fleet down to nil value was implemented some time ago. The other options for British Airways would be to put the Concorde fleet in the accounts at cost less depreciation, which would put the value in the high millions, or to use current cost, that is the amount that would be needed to replace the fleet at today's prices which would run into billions. Three vastly differing values for exactly the same aeroplane.

The approach which is adopted for fixed asset valuations can clearly have quite an impact on a company's accounts. The choice is therefore not taken lightly and will depend as much on the company's own requirements as it will on the overriding obligation to show a true and fair view of the business. It is also quite complex because not only must a decision be taken on the valuation basis but also on the consequent rates of depreciation which must be charged.

The advantages of beefing up the balance sheet through an upward fixed asset revaluation must be weighed against the increased depreciation which will accrue and which must be charged each year to the profit and loss account. A careful juggling of valuation and depreciation will usually allow a company to arrive at a combination which will maximize the impact on the balance sheet and minimize its effect on the profit and loss account.

So far the term 'fixed assets' has been used fairly loosely. It would be wrong however to assume that all the assets which fall into this category are suitable targets for manipulation in both directions. Certainly depreciation rates can be used to influence in a downward direction the stated value of all fixed assets but upward revaluations can only be applied to certain types. In the main it is land and buildings which are the most appropriate candidates for revaluations.

The wish to reflect increasing property prices is understandable. However, the question of identifying and quantifying those increases in order to reflect them in the accounts is another matter. Again, those who have had any involvement with the property market will know that the valuations which are attributed to a property can vary quite considerably, and that they can fluctuate quite sharply over a relatively short period of time.

The number of different valuations equates exactly with the number of estate agents who are asked to pass an opinion. As house sellers are acutely aware, there is only one real valuation and that is the price at which a buyer is prepared to part with his hard-earned cash. The exact value is therefore easy to determine when a sale takes place but it is not difficult to see that there is room for considerable flexibility when the valuation of a company's assets is carried out purely for academic accounting purposes.

So broad are the valuation bands in the real world that there is no need for a company to retreat to fantasy land in order to come up with a figure for its land and buildings which meets its needs. It would be wrong to suggest that the surveying profession is failing in its duties to provide fair and independent advice. Rather it is the vagaries of the property market which allows such varying valuations. That said, there have been cases where a company has had a property revaluation carried out by one firm of surveyors and when this has failed to produce the anticipated results another revaluation has been immediately summoned from a different firm so that more appropriate values can be established. Such extreme cases are the exception rather than the rule but while one surveyor's opinion continues to be as good as the next surveyor's opinion there is always going to be a lot of room for manoeuvre.

Property is the most obvious candidate for revaluation as it does not have exclusive rights. Other fixed assets can also be the target for a rethink on what they are worth. This is particularly worrying when companies are a little selective about their treatment of fixed assets. By picking and choosing which assets are to be revalued and when this is to be done a company retains much greater control over the figures it reports.

For some companies, the policies on fixed asset valuations seem to owe more to the rules of stud poker than to accounting conventions. The name of the game is to give away enough to maintain interest but never so much that people will know exactly what you have. As with all card games there will be those who do not play by the rules. Fixed asset revaluations are, therefore, something akin to the ace up the sleeve which can be produced when the game is not going your way. That ace will be played only as an act of last resort which is why it is not unusual to see fixed asset revaluations featuring prominently as part of a defence against an unwanted take-over.

It is a fairly standard tactic, these days, for a company which is on the wrong end of a hostile bid miraculously to come up with a new revaluation for its fixed assets which demonstrates quite conclusively that the predator has grossly underestimated the value of the business and is merely attempting to pick it up on the cheap. So common is the tactic that its impact is often undermined. However, there is no doubt that asset valuations still remain one of the most contentious areas of debate during take-over battles.

The inconsistency has already been identified by the Accounting Standards Board as an area for consideration. In a discussion paper dealing with the role of valuation in financial reporting the ASB set out radical proposals to enforce companies to revalue regularly most of the assets shown in their accounts. Full revaluations would have to be done every five years with desktop or partial revaluations undertaken on an annual basis. The aim would be to introduce some consistency. It would prevent undervaluation and also discourage overvaluation.

The old historical cost convention has already been discredited by the significant number of revaluations. A survey conducted by the ASB showed that 70 per cent of companies already revalue operating properties and that 83 per cent of these had done so in the previous five years. By the same token current cost accounting which was at the heart of the downfall of the old Accounting Standards Committee is too difficult to deal with. The attempts by the profession to introduce some form of inflation accounting failed miserably. It is a costly and some would say misleading form of accounting. The ASB is therefore led to modify the current regime by introducing a degree of consistency whereby current values are introduced into the balance sheet on a regular basis.

The problem for industry is one of cost and subjectivity, although it has to be said that the rules as currently constructed allow for a high degree of flexibility. GEC, for instance, has steadfastly valued its fixed assets, including property, in the balance sheet at cost. Many other companies will include their assets, and particularly property assets, at the revalued amount.

Be it a part of bid defence, an attempt to beef up the balance sheet or a genuine effort to reflect true value to the business, fixed asset valuations will always present opportunities for creative accounting. These opportunities are not restricted to the balance sheet since the consequent charge to the profit and loss account for depreciation will also be affected.

The implications for the profit and loss account are also important with regard to the amount of profit which is taken on the disposal of an asset. This has been tackled by the ASB and inconsistencies have been ironed out. Using the example below it is clear just where those inconsistencies arose.

Take three companies, A, B and C, which all buy identical fixed assets for £20,000 on 1 January 1986. The estimated life of this type of asset is ten years after which it will have no residual value. Company A carries out no revaluations of the asset but on 31 December 1988 both B and C decide that it is then worth £28,000. On 31 December 1990, Company C carries out a further revaluation of the asset and estimates that on that date it is worth £30,000. A year later on 31 December 1991 all three companies sell their assets for an identical price of £30,000. The transactions will be recorded in the books of A, B and C as follows:

	Company A (£000)	Company B (£000)	Company C (£000)
Cost 1.1.86	20	20	20
Depreciation to 31.12.88	(6)	(6)	(6)
	14	14	14
Revaluation 31.12.88	–	14	14
Net book value 31.12.88	14	28	28
Depreciation to 31.12.90	(4)	(8)	(8)
	10	20	20
Revaluation 31.12.90	–	–	10
Net book value 31.12.90	10	20	30
Depreciation to 31.12.91	(2)	(4)	(6)
Net book value 31.12.91	8	16	24
Sales proceeds	30	30	30
Net book value 31.12.91	(8)	(16)	(24)
Surplus on disposal	22	14	6

The differing approaches to valuations of the assets also affect the total charge made to the profit and loss account over the period. The total effect is summarized thus:

	Company A (£000)	Company B (£000)	Company C (£000)
Surplus on disposal	22	14	6
Total depreciation charged	(12)	(18)	(20)
Net effect	10	(4)	(14)

The illustration assumes that the surpluses on the revaluations carried out by Companies B and C are incorporated in the balance sheet through a revaluation reserve. Similarly an element of the surplus on disposal will be dealt with through the same reserve as it switches from being 'unrealized' to 'realized'. It also assumes that asset disposals are treated as part of profits for the year rather than being disclosed separately.

It is apparent that the differing valuation approaches result in widely differing impacts on the profit and loss account. Although Company A receives no benefit to its balance sheet by retaining the asset at cost throughout the period, it actually increases its profit by £10,000. Both Companies B and C, however, show reductions in their reported profits. It therefore appears that there is a strong incentive for a business not to incorporate asset revaluations. Certainly the balance sheet does not benefit, but reported profits will appear that much better. Also, if a company is judged on the basis of the return that it makes on assets, there is a clear advantage in sticking with historical cost since the business will be reporting higher profits on lower asset values. Such management and performance accounting can, however, be dangerous since it is liable to distort the real level of achievement.

The inequality of the differing approaches has not been lost on the creative accountant. Before the introduction of FRS3 many companies, rather than suffer from a reduction in reported profits, overcame the problem by including their realized revaluation surplus as part of the profit on disposal of the asset.

The illustration opposite shows how this approach served to equalize the net effect on reported profits for the period that the asset is held.

By adopting this approach both Companies B and C catch up with Company A in the year of disposal. In doing so, however, they will alter the level of profit which is reported at the time of the sale, since they will also include an element of the realized revaluation surplus. This reflects the different amounts of

	Company A	Company B	Company C
	(£000)	(£000)	(£000)
Surplus on disposal	22	14	6
Realized revaluation surplus	–	14	24
Depreciation charged	(12)	(18)	(24)
Net effect	10	10	10

depreciation which have been charged as a result of the changes in the value attributed to the asset. The profit reported on the disposals will therefore be:

	Company A	Company B	Company C
	(£000)	(£000)	(£000)
Surplus on disposal	22	14	6
Realized revaluation surplus	–	14	24
Reported profit on disposal	22	28	30

Although the net effect on all three companies is exactly the same over the period, the timing of the reporting of the profits differs. The policy that a business adopts is likely to be influenced, then, by the profits profile which is most appropriate to its particular needs.

It is to deal with these problems that the ASB has ordered companies to calculate property disposal profits by reference to the carrying value rather than cost. This prevents companies from using transfers from the revaluation reserve effectively to write the property back to its original cost. In future the revaluation surpluses must be identified in the statement of recognized gains and losses. They cannot then be written back at the time of disposal.

So far, the creative accounting aspects of dealing with fixed assets have concentrated very much on revaluing assets upwards. However, there is also some scope for manipulating reported results by reducing the value at which assets are carried. It may not seem to be a particularly sensible thing to do; after all, there does not seem to be much merit in deliberately understating what a business is worth. This might only encourage a take-over bid or for quoted companies result in some weakness in the share price.

That may well be so but as a short-term tactical measure, the writing down of fixed assets can be quite useful. It is perhaps most appropriate for businesses which have recently suffered from a difficult trading time. This may have been due to specific difficulties within an industry, more general economic problems as witnessed in the recent recession or simply because of bad and inefficient management. For these companies the main objective may simply be one of survival. The general downturn in the trading performance will probably have been accompanied by a large element of dissatisfaction either from shareholders, the company's bankers or indeed both. They will want to see change and to help them get it they may insist on a new team of management which is charged with the specific responsibility of restoring the company's fortunes. The risks for such a team are high. Failure to accomplish the task may result in a loss of credibility which may restrict the opportunities for future gainful employment. At the same time the rewards are equally attractive. The increasing use of share option schemes for these crisis and rescue management teams can mean that they have the chance to become very wealthy if they knock a business back into shape. It is the size of those rewards and the cost of failure which create a climate which encourages creative accounting.

It is a climate in which there are considerable benefits from starting out with a low asset base and gradually building up. The smaller the level of assets at the start, the more pronounced subsequent increases will be. Similarly the lower the profits at the beginning the easier it will be to improve on them.

Imagine a company, which, through no fault of the management, has produced some poor trading figures.

Business has simply been bad. However, the company's
bankers blame the management and threaten to withdraw
credit facilities if there isn't a change at the top. Reluctantly
the non-executive directors bow to this threat of imminent
liquidation and replace the senior management team with some
fresh blood. The change-over takes place just after the year end
although there had been sufficient time for the old management to draw up draft accounts. The company has fixed assets
with a book value of £100 million and depreciation is charged
at the rate of 10 per cent a year. The business is making profits
after all charges, but before tax and depreciation, of £15
million. The new team takes over and on examining the
business decides that the fixed assets are worth only half the
amount at which they are stated in the accounts. They
immediately decide, therefore, on a substantial write-down in
asset values which because of its nature will be treated as an
exceptional item and therefore may be excluded from what the
City thinks is the most relevant measure of profitability. The
accounts of the old and new management would be published
as follows:

	Old	New
	(£m)	(£m)
Trading profit	15	15
Depreciation	(10)	(5)
Headline pre-tax profit	5	10
Exceptional item	–	(50)
Net fixed asset value	90	45

The impact of the accounting changes brought about by the
new management is swift and sudden. At a stroke the company
doubles its headline pre-tax profits. Although the asset value
attributable to the business is halved the reported return earned
on those fixed assets is increased from 5.6 per cent under the

old management to 22.2 per cent under the new team. It is a huge difference and gives the immediate impression that the new management has got the business under control and is steering it along the road to recovery. That impression is of course misleading. The old management could have obtained exactly the same result by adopting a similar accounting policy. To the outside world it appears, however, as if the new management is at last making the assets sweat. The only sweating in fact is done by the creative accountants as they pore over the books in search of other ways to portray the new management in a more favourable light and at the same time make the financial performance under the old management look as bleak as possible.

It is a common occurrence nowadays for new management teams to make substantial provisions and write-downs in the year of their arrival in an effort to get all the bad news out of the way at one fell swoop. That bad news can be blamed on the ineptitude of their predecessors, so although the company may report a horrendous set of figures, the new management are free from any responsibility for the catastrophe. More important, from their point of view, the path has been cleared for the company to be rationalized and restructured, if such things are needed, without incurring unfortunate blots on the financial performance by which they will be judged.

It must also be remembered that having written the assets down, the new management is not committed to maintaining them in the books at that level. The right to revalue those same assets in an upward direction is not forgone. When the time is right the values could be reinstated with all the benefits which were explored earlier. As time passes, the new management would be able to restore the asset base which it had so deliberately eroded when it first took office. This is not to say that the improvement in the business is purely artificial and simply the work of slick accounting practices. For the new team to prove its real worth it will have to wring out some genuine improvements in the company's operations. However, what this creative accounting does is to exaggerate the extent of that improvement and contrast the performance between old and new more starkly.

Such massive depreciation write-downs against fixed assets tend to be limited to the type of situations envisaged above. However, there may well be instances when a company wants to accelerate the depreciation it charges. The rate which is chosen is purely arbitrary, as is the method which is adopted, so the opportunities for dabbling with depreciation are legion. Indeed it is very difficult for a company's auditors to argue with the basis which is ultimately adopted since the depreciation charge is little more than a stab in the dark at assessing the natural wear and tear which any asset incurs. Take the company car for instance. It may be depreciated equally over four years at 25 per cent a year. Yet as all new car owners know, the biggest slab of depreciation is incurred the minute the new vehicle is driven proudly off the garage forecourt.

It should not be assumed of course that assets will be depreciated in the first place. There are many assets dotted around the country where the company's management feel that there is no need to make any adjustment for wear and tear. The argument is that if asset values are constantly rising why is there any need to depreciate? It is not an argument which sits well with the recent property slump and tends to overlook the fact that buildings do need a degree of refurbishment. It is debatable whether the non-depreciation of assets can be tolerated in the long term.

Given that the depreciation charge can never be more than a rough approximation of the decline in an asset's value it is quite simple for a company to make gentle adjustments to the amount which is actually charged, either by reviewing asset lives, altering assumptions on residual values or adjusting the actual rate applied.

Changes in asset lives can have a material impact on the depreciation charge for the year. Yet because this is a matter of great subjective judgement it is impossible to argue with a company's decision to make a change. They should know better than anyone whether a particular asset will now last for

twenty years rather than ten. The effect, however, is significant
in that the consequence of such an alteration is to halve the
depreciation charge. Similarly, if the residual asset is increased
it can again have a material impact on the annual charge to the
profit and loss account.

Courtesy of some subtle and careful planning, the depreciation charge can allow a business to take advantage of the years
of plenty by increasing the amount which is reported in order
to have something in reserve for the years of famine. Once
again it is simply a question of smoothing the profits.

Perhaps the only limiting factor on the amount of
depreciation which can be charged is the level of the fixed
assets against which to charge it. The classification of what
assets are deemed to be fixed is, therefore, highly significant
and as is often the case there are sufficient areas which are
suitably grey in colour to allow a company some flexibility.

The argument is essentially that of what is capital and what is
revenue expenditure. This is a question of particular interest
to the Inland Revenue since the answer can have a bearing on a
company's tax liability. The general rule is that fixed assets are
those which the company intends to use on a continuing basis.
This is clear enough but there are a number of areas where the
basic rule is open to interpretation.

For instance, although company law does not allow
businesses to capitalize research costs, in special circumstances
it does permit the capitalization of development costs. But
where does research stop and development begin? The line
between the two is thin and not clearly drawn and even when
the division is established the amount which can be capitalized
includes staff costs, material costs, overheads and even
depreciation itself. Clearly the more a company can classify
as development expenditure the less it will have to charge
against profits for the year. Not only is the charge to profits
reduced but it is also deferred, since the development costs
as capitalized need not be amortized until such time as the
programme moves into commercial production. Once again a
company is presented with an excellent opportunity to control

its flow of profits. The amount of development expenditure actually charged will rely to a large extent on the company's internal cost allocations structure and, within reason, it should be possible to turn the flow on and off in order to influence the reported profits in any particular year.

A second grey area is that relating to the treatment of computer software which has become an important aspect of almost all commercial life. In the early days the tendency was to write such costs off straight to the profit and loss account when they were incurred. However, as these costs grew both in frequency and in magnitude there has been a similar increase in the number of companies looking to mitigate the impact by treating the expenditure as being capital in nature. Arguments can be presented for treating computer software as either fixed or intangible assets depending on how it was acquired or developed. Again the company can exercise some control over these costs with the decision being based more on its own needs than the rather vague criteria which must be examined in reaching that decision.

A further item which has grown in popularity as a source of capitalization is the interest which is incurred on borrowings raised to finance the construction of a fixed asset. The food retailing sector, with its huge expenditure on store development programmes, has led the way. Both Tesco and J. Sainsbury capitalize interest on store development which gives them a seemingly unfair profits advantage over those chains which can afford to finance stores development out of internally generated cash funds. More of this, though, in the chapter dealing with cash and borrowings which highlights the problems which can arise from this approach.

Fixed assets then are pliable, flexible and mobile. Everything, then, except fixed!

9. Cash and Borrowings

Cash is king. Ever since the barter economy gave way to one based on an exchangeable currency, money has made the world go around. It has become the lifeblood of every company. A surfeit of liquid funds is an indication of success, a surfeit of debt is an indication of failure. A business can play around as much as it likes with the value of its other assets and liabilities but when the money runs out then its days are numbered. Redundancy provisions can be charged against operating profit or as exceptional items, they can be deferred or brought forward but if the cash isn't there to pay the sacked workers their entitlement when they leave then the other issues become completely irrelevant. Income can be recognized at whatever time the company chooses but if it never actually receives the cash then it can start counting the days it has left for this world.

It is because of this importance that a company's cash presents only the most limited scope for creative accounting. However, the greater scope with debt has ensured that a standard has been required to deal with the creativity which is inspired by the very importance of the subject matter. Other areas of the balance sheet and profit and loss account are granted their opportunities for creativity because of the absence of a firm relationship between them and actual cash payments. Further, these areas are open to large amounts of subjective assessment and assumption which is clearly not available when dealing with cash. A bank will not take very kindly to a company deciding that the £1 million it owes will be written down to a mere £100,000. The only way that the £1 million can be reduced is for the company to repay its debt. Given this constraint and the clear importance of a company's liquidity it is not surprising that the scope for creative accounting is quite rightly restricted. Although companies are required under FRS1 to provide a comprehensive cash flow statement this is a document which, while a significant improvement on its predecessor, has limitations since it must always refer back to those parts of the accounts which are less clearly identified with liquid resources. This statement aside, there is little in the financial accounts to indicate the company's cash position apart from a year end on year end comparison of the cash and borrowings position. This of course has its limitations as an indicator of cash flow since the balance sheet is no more than a photograph of the company's state of affairs at a given point in time. A better indication comes from the amount of interest which has been paid or received in the year although this of course is influenced by the rates which have applied during the period. It is also distorted by the ability to capitalize some parts of the interest payments thus reducing the total actually reported.

It is this limitation on the outsiders' ability to assess the real cash flow of the business which offers one opportunity for creativity. By and large that opportunity is restricted to a subtle use of disclosure and to a lesser extent the control of cash flows which is more akin to the largely discredited window-dressing. There are of course innumerable off-balance-sheet financing schemes now available and these are discussed in greater detail in a separate chapter.

On a first glance the rules on disclosure do not offer a tremendous amount of room for manoeuvre. The basic principle laid down in the Companies Act is that no set-off between assets and liabilities is permitted. The implication is that cash balances cannot be offset against borrowings to reduce the overall group position. However, a closer analysis of the law's wording suggests that there are certain situations where some element of netting-off will be allowed. This is because the law does not actually define what it means by liability and it can be argued that a suitable definition would be one based on the amount which a company would have to pay if legal proceedings were taken against it to recover monies owing. Under that definition there will be several situations where netting-off could be allowed. These situations all assume that cash deposits and borrowings are arranged with the same bank and by the same company. Thus, cash deposited by one subsidiary could not be offset against borrowings by another unless specific criteria are met.

Netting-off will therefore be allowed in situations where cash deposited and cash borrowed are done under similar conditions such as where the relevant sums are due for payment on demand or on the same date. Group balances could be offset on consolidation in situations where all the subsidiaries agreed that they were jointly or severally liable to the bank for the amounts owing and similarly the bank accepted that it had joint and several liability to repay deposits.

The benefits of netting off for a company is that the total level of debt which the group has is masked by the inclusion of cash balances. So a company which has not used netting off before might be able to do so on a selective basis in a particular year in order to give the impression that it has not been borrowing as much money as would otherwise be indicated in its financial statements.

However, netting off has severe limitations. When the City is assessing a group's level of gearing it bases its calculations on the company's net borrowings position anyway. There is no immediate benefit then in terms of influencing this all-important ratio which is regarded very much as an indication of financial stability. The company must therefore rely on the timing of its cash payments and receipts if it is to succeed in manipulating its cash and borrowings position.

For companies which are highly geared, that is with large net borrowings positions, the aim will be to defer cash payments at the year end until the next accounting period. The company will defer making payments to creditors in an effort artificially to inflate the cash position. One of the favourite methods of window-dressing is to write out cheques for creditor payments but not to send the cheques out. All over the country at year end time there are large bundles of cheques sitting in finance directors' drawers waiting to be sent out. This rather unsubtle method of reducing the level of creditors while designed to present bank balances in a better light very rarely works these days. Even the most unsophisticated of auditing firms is well aware of the trick. However, variations on that scheme can still work. Providing the cheques are not actually written out then certain liabilities can be disclosed as part of creditors rather than as a bank overdraft which will clearly help the year end cash position. Any payment over which the company has an element of control is a reasonable target for deferral. These, like staff bonuses or redundancy payments, should, if possible, be delayed until the next accounting period.

The counter to this is to bring forward cash receipts into the current accounting period. This is obviously more difficult. Since many companies share common year ends it follows that if everybody is trying to delay making payments then collecting cash early is easier said than done. However, a closer than usual attention to debt collection will reap its benefits particularly if the process is stepped up two or three months rather than two or three days before the year end.

The year end cash position can also be improved by a much more ruthless approach to stock control as the accounting period draws to its inevitable conclusion. It is easy to overlook how much cash can be tied up in excessively and unnecessarily high levels of stock. A gradual run down of stocks will inevitably free up cash although care must be taken that this does not result in damaging shortages. However, such methods of improving the cash position owe more to careful and prudent management than to creative accounting.

But not all businesses have the problems of excessive gearing to cope with. Remember, a prudent level of borrowing is often looked upon as being a sign of good management. High cash balances can be regarded as a waste of a company's resources.

When similar companies are earning a return of 20 per cent on their assets and another company has large amounts of cash stashed away in the building society, then City analysts and company shareholders alike begin to wonder why. There can be an incentive then for a company to give the impression that its year end cash position is not as healthy as it really is.

The methods employed in such a situation are the exact opposite of those used when a company is trying to inflate its year end cash position. Payments are accelerated and if possible, debtors are invited to delay their payments which they will normally be happy to do. The motive does not have to derive from the wish to reduce the level of net cash disclosed in the balance sheet. It may owe more to the need to smooth out cash flows. If a company has had a year of unusually positive cash flow, perhaps because of an unavoidable delay in a particular capital investment which will not take place until the next accounting period, it may not necessarily want this distortion to be reflected in the amounts. Once again the company's objective will be to remove unusual fluctuations and demonstrate that it has a steadily improving cash flow profile. It will not want to have a one-off benefit to its net cash position in one year which will be immediately removed in the next simply as a function of the timing of a particular capital investment.

However, the year end position is not the only indicator of the company's cash flow. The interest paid or received in the year will give a further indication of the level of average borrowings. Here again there is not a tremendous amount of scope for creative accounting and the emphasis is much more on good treasury management. There are tremendous savings which can be made by a company if it keeps a close eye on the money markets and, if it has overseas transactions to deal with, then on the foreign exchange markets as well. Apart from the various money market instruments which can be used a company must also pay close attention to the way in which its borrowings are structured.

There are several ways in which the portfolio of debt can be constructed in order to reduce the level of interest payable. By combining short-term borrowings with long-term debt a company can secure both flexibility and competitive interest rates. It should also consider its capital structure. If long-term debt is threatening to get out of hand a company could reduce it by launching a rights issue. Such a move is not always welcomed by the stock market, particularly if the reason for it is cited as just debt reduction and is not linked to any other long-term strategic plan. Again, this is more in the domain of the corporate treasurer than the creative accountant.

The same is true of money market instruments such as futures and swaps which can be used as a means of either speculation or hedging. However, the money markets are highly competitive places and are no place for the casual player or inexperienced trader. Unless the company's treasury needs are big enough to justify a separate department these matters might be better left to the experts although this does not preclude simple measures such as placing large cash sums on overnight deposit. However, there have been a sufficiently high number of disasters in the derivatives and currency markets, even among big and supposedly sophisticated international companies, to caution against this arena of creativity. The benefits from internal treasury/management can be substantial but so too can the costs.

Sophisticated treasury management is not a secure means of manipulating cash resources. However, that has not stopped companies from resorting to sophisticated capital instruments as a way to present their overall financial position in a more favourable light. These instruments grew increasingly popular throughout the eighties and were designed essentially to allow companies to secure access to funds which could be classified as equity rather than debt. It is a quite crucial distinction, given the importance of gearing to those who have to make a judgement about a company and its prospects.

The accounting treatment of these complex capital instruments has vexed the Accounting Standards Board which has produced a set of rules designed to clarify the issue. FRS4 dealing with Capital Instruments sets out to ensure that financial statements provide a clear, coherent and consistent treatment in particular with regard to their classification as debt, non-equity shares or equity shares. These are important distinctions and it is not surprising that the ASB's ruling has not met with universal support.

To give some indication of the importance of this area it is instructive to examine some of the capital instruments which are available.

One of the most controversial has been Auction Market Preferred Shares, or AMPS as they are more commonly known, which were devised in the United States. They are preference shares which are entitled to a dividend which is not fixed but set through an auction process. The shares are transferred at a fixed price to the investor who will accept the lowest dividend. The auction takes place regularly and if there are no bidders then the shares remain in the ownership of the current holder and the dividend is increased to what is known as the default rate which is calculated by a prescribed formula.

The attraction for investors is that the AMPS will provide a return in excess of that which can be secured in other money markets. For the company the attraction was that prior to FRS4 AMPS were classified as equity rather than debt; yet at the same time they do not dilute the interest of existing shareholders since they are not entitled to the dividend on ordinary shares which is paid in the normal course of business.

However, the attraction of AMPS has been in some cases quite short-lived and a number of companies have ended up with severe problems as a consequence. It is not possible, either, to disguise the presence of AMPS in the accounts. Under FRS4 they must be identified separately as non-equity shares which immediately highlights both their presence and their limitations.

Where the ASB ran into more controversial territory was with its ruling on how convertible debt should be treated. Although convertible bonds have many guises the basic principle is the same in that the debt converts at some point in time to equity. There was clearly therefore a desire for companies to treat this convertible debt as equity. The arguments for this treatment attracted some support particularly because in some cases conversion to equity will be clearly anticipated. However, it was not enough to persuade the ASB to amend its tough line designed to force companies to treat convertible issues as debt rather than equity and it chose to reject the argument that the option to convert was a reason to include these instruments as part of shareholder funds. FRS4 demands that conversion of debt should not be anticipated.

This has cast a doubt, therefore, over the effectiveness of convertible capital bond issues by a special purpose subsidiary incorporated outside the UK. Interest is paid periodically and prior to conversion they may be exchanged for shares of the subsidiary which at the option of the bondholder are either immediately redeemed or immediately exchanged for ordinary shares of the parent. The bonds and the payments in respect of the shares of the subsidiary are guaranteed by the parent. The parent meanwhile retains the right to issue convertible redeemable preference shares in substitution for the bonds should it so choose.

There is little doubt that in the accounts of the subsidiary the bonds should be treated as debt since the obligation to pay interest is what the ASB regards as an obligation to transfer economic benefits. At the group level it could be argued that the bonds represent non-equity shares since the parent has the option to issue convertible preference shares in substitution for the bonds. However, this is rejected by the ASB and it insists that the bonds be treated as convertible debt.

Convertible debt with a premium put option has also been a popular form of fund raising. This is essentially debt which has an option for the holder to demand redemption either at maturity or some earlier date for an amount that is in excess of the amount originally received for the debt. These schemes were particularly popular with companies because they appeared to offer a low cost form of finance, since when they were launched it was envisaged that the redemption premium option would never be exercised.

The premium put option guaranteed the investor a higher return than would have been received on an identical bond without the option. Indeed this was at the heart of their popularity with investors. However, it created an uncertainty about the ultimate action of the investor which was impossible to predict. That depended on the value of the shares at conversion compared with the cash receivable, including the premium, on exercise of the option. It is this uncertainty over conversion which has persuaded the ASB that these instruments should be treated as a liability and disclosed separately.

The same treatment applies to a variation on this theme which is convertible debt with enhanced interest. As an alternative to the premium described above the debt will contain an undertaking that the interest will be increased at a date in the future. At the time of the issue, however, it is uncertain whether the debt will be converted before the enhanced interest is payable. This enhanced interest will tend to equate to the returns which investors might receive on other non-convertible forms of debt. It therefore creates uncertainty about conversion which under the ASB's rules condemns the instrument to treatment as a liability.

There is less debate over the treatment of deep discounted bonds which carry a low nominal rate of interest or in the case of zero coupon bonds none at all. They are therefore issued at a discount to the value at which they will be redeemed. These bonds must be disclosed as liabilities. More interesting is the treatment of the finance costs which will be covered later in the chapter.

Income bonds are those where interest is only payable when the issuer has sufficient reported profits, after allowing for interest on other kinds of debt, to make the payment. If profits are insufficient to make a payment the issuer is not in default and no additional rights accrue to the bondholder although the interest due may be cumulative. The bonds will be redeemed at a fixed price at a fixed date. That obligation to redeem taken with the requirement to make interest payments even though they are dependent on profits is sufficient to ensure that they must be treated as a liability.

Sometimes loan agreements will not specify the level of interest payments, which will be calculated instead by reference to a formula which may well refer to the base rate or some other form of indexing. Again there is little doubt about the treatment of this form of debt as a liability. More pertinent is the treatment of finance costs.

In cases of limited recourse debt, where in the event of default the lender has the ability to secure repayment by enforcing his rights against a particular security which is identified in the loan agreement, the nature of the borrowings is different from that normally associated with debt. However, the ASB still insists that the debt be treated as a liability and that the notes should disclose the nature of the arrangement. There are situations where the value of the security may fall to such an extent that the company is better off to default on the loan and hand over the security to the lender, but these circumstances are likely to be rare and unusual so should have no influence on the accounting treatment.

With perpetual debt the argument has been advanced that because the amount of the loan is never repayable it should not be reflected in the balance sheet. That argument is rejected by the ASB on the grounds that the obligation to pay interest is an obligation to transfer economic benefits and hence the debt is a liability. With repackaged perpetual debt, where the loan carries interest at a relatively high rate for a number of years and then bears no further charge, the ASB again argues that it should be disclosed as a liability. The substance of the arrangement, it says, is that the debt is repaid over the early years of the loan. The actual interest payments are allocated between interest and repayment and reflected in a steady reduction of the principal of the loan to an extent that it is written off over the period in which payments are made.

With subordinated loans the lender accepts that his rights are not as great as other creditors. This subordination can take a number of forms although this is irrelevant to the treatment of the loan since the obligation to repay remains and it must therefore be shown as a liability.

One final instrument to consider is the participating preference share. These are similar to other preference shares except that they are entitled in addition to a fixed dividend to a proportion of the dividends paid on equity shares. Because this entitlement to share in profits is restricted these instruments should be treated as non-equity shares and disclosed accordingly.

The main thrust of the ASB's rules is to prevent companies from artificially reducing the liabilities which are recognized in the balance sheet. Similarly they are designed to ensure that investors can make a distinction between bona-fide equity and that which is non-equity. To that extent the rules on complex capital instruments must be regarded as a success. However, there is a lingering problem which is only just beginning to emerge. Already a number of schemes are being devised which allow companies to use complex capital instruments but to do so in a way in which they are treated as part of minority interests rather than on the face of the group's balance sheet. Just as the rules are in their infancy so too are the schemes devised to bend them. It is an area which is bound to develop with potentially damaging consequences both for the investor and for companies which do not use these minority capital instruments prudently.

If balance sheet gearing is one tool which investors use to assess how a company is funded the profit and loss corollary of this is interest cover. This is designed to assess by what ratio profits exceed the interest payments a company must make on its borrowings.

This has been covered in detail in FRS4 and in many cases it is the allocation of finance costs associated with these capital instruments which is more important than the balance sheet treatment.

The basic rule on finance costs is that they should be recognized at a constant rate on the carrying amount of the debt. This has profound consequences in that there will not always be a correlation between the interest payment actually made and that which is charged to the profit and loss account. Over the term of the capital instrument the two will even out but there will sometimes be inconsistencies on an annual basis.

This has had the most marked effect on convertible bonds. Not only did they lose the potential to be disclosed as equity but under the new rules the associated finance costs have also been altered. This subject was first addressed by the Urgent Issues Task Force in 1991 which ruled that the supplemental interest which bondholders would sometimes be entitled to or the premium they might receive on redemption would have to be treated as part of the finance costs associated with the bonds. The effect was to increase the charges so that it was not just the coupon rate which was reflected in the profit and loss account but also a proportion of the premium which might be payable on redemption.

With deep discounted bonds which carry a low nominal rate of interest the finance charges must be increased to reflect the total payment the company must make. The finance cost will therefore be the net proceeds from the bond issue and the total payments which will have to be made up to and including redemption. These are allocated evenly over the life of the bond. Even with stepped interest bonds which involve a progressively increasing interest rate the ASB insists that the same rate is applied across the period of the bond so that a true economic rate is established.

The ASB's approach has a compelling consistency and logic to it although it does create a degree of mismatch between cash flow and reported profits which is a function of the accruals process. This is unfortunate although the aim of the ASB's thinking is to prevent understatement of interest which would allow companies to secure a more flattering interest rate cover.

However, while the ASB has made progress in dealing with the allocation of finance costs it has done little to arrest a rather crude way of reducing interest and this also involves the largest element of creative accounting. It goes under the name of capitalization of interest and over the last decade this has become a quite standard practice. Put simply a company treats the interest on that element of borrowings which are employed to finance the construction of fixed assets as part of the cost of those assets.

Some of the greatest exponents of interest capitalization are the big supermarket chains who are committed to very costly store development programmes. The nature of the competition among the big food retailers dictates that the way forward is through bigger and more expensive stores. These have gone from being supermarkets, to being hypermarkets, to being superstores, to being megastores. No one is quite sure where it will all end. The only thing that is certain is that the number of available sites is falling while the competition to secure those sites is increasing. This pushes up the asking prices and increases the development costs which the big chains must incur. This is turn pushes up the financing requirements and the interest burden.

J. Sainsbury, one of the country's leading retailers, led the way again as it became the first company to start capitalizing its interest costs on its store development programme. That lead was taken up by Tesco who also took the interest capitalization route. The benefits of this approach are considerable. First, both companies automatically increase their reported pre-tax profits. Second, some element of the interest escapes permanently a charge to the profit and loss account. This is because freehold land is not the subject of depreciation. So while the interest relating to the building will ultimately be charged against profits, albeit by a much delayed amortization cost, the interest which is allocated to the land will never actually be charged to the revenue account. Finally, by using an accounting policy which is not used by other food retailers, the likes of Sainsbury and Tesco get an unfair stock market advantage. If anything, those companies which do not capitalize interest and actually finance store development out of their own internally generated resources are penalized.

There was always a danger that this interest capitalization would get out of hand as the store expansion plans become more ambitious. In their 1994 accounts both Tesco and Sainsbury were obliged to take account of the changing world in which they operated and, to some extent, of the effect of rolling up their interest charges.

In those accounts both Tesco and Sainsbury recognized that their land and buildings no longer reflected the true value to the company and both decided to institute significant write-downs. Tesco wrote off £85 million relating to surplus land. It also started to amortize land premiums, those paid above its value with alternative usage, which cost £32.1 million in 1993/94 and had a retrospective cost of £59.4 million. The company also introduced a depreciation charge for its buildings which cost £36.4 million in 1993/94. The total of all these write-offs comes to £212.9 million. Yet the company still capitalizes interest and its fixed assets include total capitalized interest of £235.6 million. The two figures are remarkably similar.

Sainsbury for its part decided to write down the value of its properties by £282 million and also took a £59 million charge relating to provisions for losses on surplus land and stores due for closure. The total comes to £341 million. Given that interest capitalized in the year was a little under £30 million it puts the write-off in some context.

It is a technique which has its attractions but also its limitations if a company does not keep an eye on what is happening in the real world.

This is something that investors must come to their own conclusions on. They must decide whether the interest capitalization is a genuine attempt to reflect the nature of the costs incurred more fairly or merely an effort to delay bad financial news until it can be compensated for by some better news. Even when companies appear to be taking a more prudent approach to the capitalization question there is a need to be alert. A company which changes its policy to capitalizing rather than non-capitalizing interest payable may in effect be reflecting a decline in property values in part through a prior year adjustment.

Just like sin, cash flow will eventually find a company out. All that interest capitalization does is put off the day of judgement. Cash can sometimes be a very cruel king and has little mercy on those who try to abuse its power by excessive creative accounting. If ever there was a case for moderation then it is over the way that a company accounts for and discloses its cash and borrowings position. Otherwise the cry will go up: 'Cash is dead. Long live the receiver!'

10. Off-Balance-Sheet Finance

The most effective creative accounting is that which is not detected by the independent user of company accounts. The most successful and thereby the most sinister methods are those which do not appear at all in the financial statements. This branch of creative accounting is known as off-balance-sheet financing. As the name suggests this refers to the ways of raising funds for a business without reflecting those borrowings in the balance sheet.

It is not a new phenomenon but one which has grown significantly over the last decade not just in size but also in sophistication. This off-balance-sheet boom has lent an element of credibility to these methods of funding which is completely undeserved. Ironically, the initiative for the recent development of off-balance-sheet finance has not come from the companies but more from the providers of funds which have been actively marketing the schemes. This touting by the merchant banks and other financial advisers has similarities with the peddling of artificial tax avoidance schemes in the 1970s. Again the arrangements comply with the letter of the law but are contrary to its spirit. The only justification for adopting them appears to be that everybody else is doing the same thing.

This is no justification at all but it has not prevented the widespread growth in off-balance-sheet financing. The schemes also have some quite dangerous undertones in that they are being aggressively sold by some merchant banks in a way that suggests that they are actually an important financial service.

A merchant bank might, for instance, identify a company which has high borrowings which are close to the limit imposed by its articles of association. The bank then approaches the company's management and points this out and at the same time suggests an off-balance-sheet scheme which will allow the business to increase its borrowings without breaching the articles of association. There is a strong chance that the management will be more than happy to go along with the plan since this will relieve it of the embarrassment of having to go to the shareholders to ask for a change in the articles of association. This may be very convenient for the management but it undermines the very reason for those articles. They would have been included to ensure that the management which runs the company on behalf of the shareholders does not overstep the mark and commit the business to unrealistic and impractical levels of debt. Even this tenuous control that shareholders have over the management is therefore eroded.

However, it is not always the limit on borrowings power which prompts a company to seek off-balance-sheet finance. After all, the articles of association can, with shareholders' approval, be amended. That change will not help the management if the main problem for the business is that its borrowings are simply too high. The stock market is acutely aware of the dangers for a company which has high levels of debt which must be serviced. One of the crucial factors in assessing a company is its gearing, the proportion of net borrowings to shareholders' funds. When gearing becomes uncomfortably high, the stock market begins to get a little worried and the pressure is on the company to reduce the ratio.

When a company finds itself in the unfortunate position of having high gearing which cannot be reduced, or even held steady, out of internally generated funds, it is easy to see why the management might be lured into one of these artificial funding schemes. The off-balance-sheet finance may be applied to reduce existing borrowings, thus bringing down the gearing ratio, or it may be secured in order to embark on an important project or acquisition which is needed for the company's long-term future. Either way it still represents a distortion of the company's true financial position which prevents users of the accounts obtaining a full and fair understanding of its affairs and which may lead to an investment decision being taken on inappropriate grounds.

The accountancy profession has kept a watchful eye on these schemes but the standard setters found it difficult to make any meaningful wholesale assault on off-balance-sheet financing until the Accounting Standards Board came on the scene. It was concerned from the outset about off-balance-sheet financing and the potential for distortion contained therein. After lengthy deliberation it finally produced Financial Reporting Standard 5 which is called Reporting the Substance of Transactions. The title is significant. It does not tackle off-balance-sheet head on. Instead it comes at the subject very neatly from the side. In essence it is a standard based on a very simple principle which states that it is the substance of a transaction not in legal form which should be reflected in the accounts. This is a constructive way forward. Given that the main attraction of an off-balance-sheet financing scheme is that it allows a company to secure borrowings without showing the liability FRS5 has a fighting chance of catching them in its net. If the substance of a transaction is to secure borrowings then those borrowings should be shown in the balance sheet.

FRS5 is designed to cope with the proliferation of complex financing schemes which have been developed and applied over the last ten years. However, while it is the most widespread and concerted attack on off-balance-sheet finance it is not the first.

To be fair to the ASB's predecessor body the Accounting Standards Committee it was the first to dip its toe in the waters of off-balance-sheet when it produced its standard on leasing. This is a common enough and outwardly straightforward financing technique but it did have the effect of removing both assets and liabilities from the balance sheet.

The position was summed up by the ASC in its foreword to Statement of Standard Accounting Practice 21 which deals with leases and hire purchase contracts. Leasing had become a substantial source of off-balance-sheet finance and the standard was designed, just as FRS5 is, to recognize the substance rather than the legal form of a lease to ensure that leased assets and the corresponding liabilities were reflected in the accounts. The ASC said:

> When a company is leasing a substantial amount of assets instead of buying them, the effect is that, unless the leased assets and obligations are capitalized, potentially large liabilities build up off balance sheet; equally the leased assets employed are not reflected on the balance sheet. These omissions may mislead users of a company's accounts – both external users and the company's own management.

In those days it was quite a bold move by the ASC, which had not always suffered from excessive self-confidence. The conflict between the legal substance of a transaction and its practical form is not an easy one to resolve. However, the introduction of the leasing standard passed off without too much trouble despite the complexity of the subject.

It was only hindsight which explained why there was less fuss made at the time. What history has shown is that the distinction made by the standard between operating and finance leases has allowed companies sufficient flexibility to continue to use the technique to take liabilities off balance sheet. An operating lease is little more than a glorified rental agreement. It could apply to a photocopying machine or a fax machine where the asset remains the property of the lessor who takes full responsibility for it. Operating leases do not have to be reflected in the balance sheet.

Finance leases, however, are a different kettle of fish. Although the lessor may remain the technical legal owner of the asset, substantially all the risk and rewards of ownership pass to the company which has use of the asset. Finance leases are therefore required to be reflected on the balance sheet. When defining what should be classified as a finance lease

SSAP 21 says, crucially, that those leases where the present value of the minimum lease payments amounts to substantially all the fair value of the leased asset should be treated as finance leases. It goes on to say that substantially all will normally mean 90 per cent or more of the fair value. The 90 per cent figure was designed to give guidance but in effect it has become a critical cut-off point. Companies go to great lengths to ensure that the 90 per cent level is not breached. It does not matter whether the lease payments equate to 89 per cent of the fair value; if that is the figure then the finance lease treatment does not apply.

The leasing question is bound to be addressed again by the Accounting Standards Board which is conscious of the problems created by the 90 per cent cut-off level.

By way of illustration of the inconsistencies created by SSAP 21 it is instructive to look at the accounting policies of British Airways. It has a very big fleet of aircraft which are financed by a number of methods. Some are bought outright, some are leased under finance leases and some are leased more curiously under operating leases. This is rather odd. It is one thing to rent a photocopier; it is something else entirely to rent a Jumbo jet. The BA policy says:

Where assets are financed through finance leases or hire purchase agreements under which substantially all the risks and rewards of ownership are transferred to the group, the assets are treated as if they had been purchased outright. The amount included in tangible fixed assets represents the aggregate capital elements payable during the lease or hire purchase term. The corresponding obligation, reduced by the appropriate portion of lease or hire purchase payments made is included in creditors. The amount included in tangible fixed assets is depreciated on the basis described in the preceding paragraphs and the interest element of lease or hire purchase payments made is included in interest payable in the profit and loss account. Payments under all other lease arrangements are charged to the profit and loss account in equal amounts over the period of the lease. In respect of aircraft, operating lease arrangements allow the Group to terminate the leases after a limited period normally, every five to seven years without further material financial obligations.

The first part of the policy is an eloquent assessment of how the company deals with leases but it is the last sentence which is most significant. In essence it allows BA to fly many of its jets around the world without them ever appearing on the balance sheet. BA would argue that because they can exit the lease without material financial obligations then they are entitled to treat the leases this way and indeed they are. However, for at least five and sometimes seven years BA has clear liability to meet lease payments yet this is not reflected in the balance sheet.

Leasing will be revisited by the standard setters but their initial thrust into this arena remains with FRS5. As standards go it is remarkably concise. The objective of the standard is put quite simply to 'ensure that the substance of an entity's transactions is reported in its financial statements. The commercial effect of the transactions, and any resulting assets, liabilities, gains or losses should be faithfully represented in its financial statements.' That is fine and the actual standard itself is just eleven pages long. However, once further amplification is provided and some specific problems are dealt with the total contents of the FRS5 booklet spread to a cumbersome 137 pages.

Although the ASB wanted to keep its approach very simple and focused on broad principles it has been pressed to be more specific in its supporting documentation. This bears witness to the magnitude of the problem the ASB is facing. The problem is that while the most general principle is easy to identify it is much more difficult to see how it applies to specific transactions and schemes. Off-balance-sheet financing has no principles. It sees the law as something to be taken down and used in its favour. Its very lifeblood is in the strict interpretation of the law where the letter is much more important than the spirit.

Although off-balance-sheet finance has grown dramatically this is not to suggest that every company in the country is quietly involved in a series of devious schemes designed to disguise the fact that rather than being well endowed with liquid resources they are actually borrowed up to the hilt. The old rule that you can't fool all of the people all of the time still applies. However, there is no doubt that the flexibility of accounting rules and the rigidity of company law has offered in the past an enormous amount of scope for a business to portray its financial position in a better light.

The biggest problem with off-balance-sheet finance is its lack of visibility. It is impossible for investors to make a proper judgement of a company's underlying financial position and performance. Many of the schemes which have been adopted have been well managed and prudently structured. They are seen in the context of the overall funding requirements of the group and in fact investors have little to worry about. The problem is the investors would probably like just a little more reassurance on this subject. If it is not a problem why hide it? Off-balance-sheet finance may be useful in ironing out short-term fluctuations in the company's performance. But what if all it does is defer short-term problems to the medium term and stack up quite significant difficulties for the long term? It must be remembered that off-balance-sheet finance, like any other kind of borrowing, has to be repaid eventually. If a business is unable to meet its commitments be they on the balance sheet, off the balance sheet or underneath the balance sheet, then it does not matter how creative or complex a particular scheme is, those liabilities will have to be met.

The worry for investors is that by failing to disclose the full facts about its funding methods a company which indulges in matters off balance sheet is effectively passing the right to decide on its future prospects to the providers of the finance. Investors, creditors and others who rely on published financial data are being deprived of the full and fair information which is essential for making an informed decision.

As always, though, off-balance-sheet financing is a two-edged sword. While it may appear to be a superficial device which simply misleads the outside world about a company's true financial position at a given point in time, it can also be seen as a crucial provider of breathing space. If a company does have genuinely short-term financial problems which can be comfortably resolved in the fullness of time it is understandable that it would wish to deal with them in a tactful, subtle and unobtrusive fashion. The last thing it wants to do is create unjustified panic and undue concern which may lead to a loss of trust or credibility. Stability and confidence are important. It could be argued that their value to a business cannot be underestimated and if off-balance-sheet finance is the way to maintain such intangible assets then so be it. However, a more compelling argument is that the solution to this problem is to change people's understanding of and response to the short-term difficulties rather than to hide them through off-balance-sheet financing.

Leaving the moral issues aside for the time being, there is another difficulty with off-balance-sheet financing and that is pinpointing the specific ways in which it is applied. There is an understandable conspiracy of silence between those who provide this form of financing and those who receive it. Both the givers and the takers have a lot to lose but even more to gain. Like pornography, it is smutty and nasty but there are tremendous financial rewards to be had. The various schemes, therefore, go unpublicized. However, as they have become more widespread it is now possible to identify those which are in common use. Indeed the ASB provides analysis of how some of the more obvious schemes might be dealt with in practice.

The starting point for many schemes is the essential assets which a company needs to carry on its business. This is why leasing proved so popular and so successful as a source of invisible finance. On the one hand the lessee needs the asset to allow the business to function, and on the other hand the lessor has guaranteed collateral in that it retains the ultimate ownership of that asset. This is the basic principle which underpins the 'consignment stock' method of off-balance-sheet finance.

The scheme is particularly appropriate to those businesses which effectively act as sales agents for a manufacturing company. The most obvious candidate is car dealerships. The manufacturer has a vested interest in selling vehicles but knows full well that the only genuine sale is one to the end user and not merely a delivery to the agent. The financing cost for the dealer of maintaining his stock of vehicles can be prohibitively high. Therefore, the consignment stock method of financing is brought into play.

Imagine the relationship between a car manufacturer and a dealer. Both share the same common interests but at the same time have to maintain their business dealings on a relatively commercial basis. Enter now the consignment stock approach to off-balance-sheet financing. Under the scheme, stock is supplied by the manufacturer to the dealer on consignment. The full payment is not made on delivery but only falls due when the stock is sold. Arrangements may vary but a payment will only be made either immediately on sale or at some time shortly thereafter. However, although the manufacturer is clearly interested in ensuring that the dealer makes that crucial sale it is not prepared to take the full brunt of the risks and financing of the stock without some recompense.

This might take the form of a deposit which the dealer is obliged to make to the manufacturer. More often than not it will be linked to the dealer's past record of vehicle sales. It is a reasonable arrangement since it eases the manufacturer's cash flow and at the same time provides a tangible incentive for the dealer to get on with the business of selling cars. Otherwise the manufacturer runs the risk of getting involved in what is little more than a very costly sale or return system of retailing. This deposit secures the dealer's right to obtain vehicles on consignment. However, the amounts of money will not be insignificant and for the dealer will represent substantial liquid resources which are permanently tied up with the manufacturer. Clearly that deposit has to be financed and this is where the consignment scheme really begins to take effect.

Normally the deposit would be funded out of borrowings which involves not just interest but may also divert funds from other parts of the business. Therefore, the manufacturer agrees to a scheme whereby it waives the deposit in return for a monthly waiver fee. This ensures that the car manufacturer retains an element of cash flow but, more importantly, it has great benefits for the dealer. The money which would have been permanently tied up in the deposit is immediately liberated. The waiver fee can be paid for out of the dealer's own cash flow which is much less of a burden.

In effect the manufacturer is financing the dealer's trading stock. However, that stock will not appear in the dealer's accounts and more importantly neither will the 'loan' which would otherwise have been necessary to ensure a constant supply of stock. The dealer is therefore free to seek further finance from its bank, should it so need, without the encumbrance of the deposit hanging over its shoulders.

Clearly there is an advantage in this arrangement for both parties. After all, the dealer and the manufacturer are working towards the same goal in that a sale of the car is the desired objective. The assumption is that the manufacturer has sufficient confidence in the dealer's operations to justify the financing it is effectively providing. The dangers with this form of off-balance-sheet financing are more related to the distortions in the dealer's true position when it is dealing with its own bankers or when it is being compared to another dealer which does not have the benefits of the same type of financing.

There are a number of variations on this broad theme but the basic principles will be the same. The question posed under FRS5 is whether or not the dealer should account for the stock as an asset and also recognize the corresponding liability. Under the standard where it is concluded that the stock is in substance an asset of the dealer it should be recognized as such on the dealer's balance sheet, together with the corresponding liability to the manufacturer. Any deposit with the manufacturer should be deducted from the liability and the excess classified as a trade creditor. Where it is concluded that the stock is not in substance an asset of the dealer then it and the liability are excluded. Any deposit should be included under other debtors.

The difficulty comes in deciding what is the substance of the transaction. FRS5 gives a number of factors which should be taken into account in reaching the decision. Indications that the stock is not an asset of the dealer at delivery are as follows:

- Manufacturer can require the dealer to return stock or transfer it to another dealer without compensation;
- penalty paid by the dealer to prevent returns and transfers of stock made at the manufacturer's request;
- dealer has unfettered right to return stock to the manufacturer without penalty and actually exercises that right;
- manufacturer bears obsolescence risk;
- stock transfer price charged by manufacturer is based on manufacturer's list price at the date of legal transfer of title;
- manufacturer bears slow movement risk.

The indications that the stock is an asset of the dealer at delivery tend to reflect the opposite. So factors to consider here are:

- Manufacturer cannot require return or transfer of stock;
- financial incentives given for returns or transfers at the manufacturer's request;
- dealer has no right to return stock or is commercially compelled not to exercise its right of return;
- dealer bears obsolescence risks and slow movement risks;
- stock transfer price is based on manufacturer's list price at time of delivery.

This amplification helps with interpretation of the standard but you cannot help but think that these are just the kinds of question which might have been legitimately posed by the auditors. FRS5 does not comment on how many factors have to be ticked before the stock must be accounted for on a balance sheet. If the arrangements have characteristics which appear in both lists the ultimate decision remains the matter of judgement that it was always going to be. The danger here is that the ASB is being forced to be more prescriptive than it really wants to be. As we have seen with the leasing standard, once any kind of measurement is set in stone it becomes an immediate target for avoidance. A standard which is based on attacking principles becomes altogether less relevant once it gets too bogged down with detail.

That is a problem for the auditing profession which is charged with acting as the ultimate arbiter of the judgements which are made. Auditors will tend to be more sympathetic to schemes like consignment stock where the off-balance-sheet financing is being provided almost as part of the normal working relationship between customer and supplier. It could be argued that this funding is a natural extension of that relationship and therefore acceptable since it is little more than pragmatic commercial practice. The finance is not provided by way of hard cash; it simply releases funds which the dealer can then apply elsewhere in the business. However, the bulk of off-balance-sheet financing arrangements bear little relationship to commercial reality. They are just ways of providing cash which will not appear anywhere in the company's accounts as borrowings.

Again, a business's stock and work in progress provide the ideal starting point for such schemes. The 'artificial sale of stock' arrangement, as the name implies, relies heavily on the company's inventory for its success. It is particularly appropriate for businesses where the stock, or work in progress, must be retained for several years before it can be sold. A whisky distiller, or fine wine producer, might find the artificial sale method useful since the products, especially those of the former, must be laid down for some time before they are ready for onward sale to the consumer. The financing costs involved can be extremely heavy. It is not the simple storage costs which are the problem but more the cash-flow time-lag involved. The company incurs massive production costs in distilling the whisky but then has to wait several years before these can be recovered when the cash received from its sale is received.

For well-established whisky producers, where there is a constant ebb and flow of some stocks being laid down and others taken out on maturity for distribution and sale, cash-flow time-lag would be expected to have been absorbed in a production cycle which stretches back into the dim and distant past. This may well appear to be the case but the fact remains that this financing cost of maturing stocks is always there and becomes much more pronounced when the business runs into temporary difficulties. The problems which have hit the British whisky industry are well known. Over-capacity has brought over-supply which has been translated into distress selling of stocks on wafer-thin margins, or even at a loss, which has put some of the distillers under a lot of pressure.

Under these conditions it is easy to see why a company might want to resort to off-balance-sheet financing. Traditional lines of credit may well be difficult to extend since the banking community will be fully aware of the industry's problems and could therefore be reluctant to grant further borrowings to a business which has a balance sheet which might already appear to have an uncomfortable level of gearing.

It puts the company in something of a Catch 22 position since the borrowings might be needed not to finance the laying down of further stocks but rather to invest in new capital equipment which is needed to bring efficiencies to the production process. That investment may be essential if the company is to maintain its long-term competitiveness and thus ensure its survival but will be impossible to finance unless the banks take a relaxed and confident view of its prospects.

Enter, then, the artificial sale of stock scheme. Under this arrangement the company sells its stock to a finance company. The disposal can be accounted for as a sale at that time but it is not a genuine sale since the company will retain an option to repurchase the stock at a future date. It is an option which it will most certainly want to exercise. After all, the finance company is in the business of finance and the distilling company is in the business of distilling. The sale is clearly artificial since the stock will not usually leave the company's premises and will happily get on with the business of maturing blissfully unaware that its owner is now somebody completely different.

The repurchase price will of course be higher than the original selling price. It could be based on the market price at the time of resale, on the assumption that this has been rising, or more likely on the original sales price adjusted upwards for the rolled-up interest which has accrued during the period of ownership. So when the whisky has matured and is ready for consumption by the eager consumer, the buy-back option is expected, the finance house is repaid and life continues as if nothing untoward has happened.

The difference between the original price at which the stock was sold to the finance house and the price at which it is repurchased is in effect a financing charge which replaces the interest which the company would have had to pay had it been funding the stock, while it matured, out of externally generated borrowings. The financing charge is, however, likely to be a little higher than that incurred using commercial interest rates.

The impact on the finances of the distilling company as a consequence of this transaction is considerable. There are implications both for the recognition of the sale and the attributed cost of that sale. More importantly for the company, it has the free use of the funds raised through the artificial sale of the stock for the duration of the whisky's maturity period. The funds can be applied in whatever direction the company wishes either to meet short-term cash-flow shortfalls or to finance crucial investment projects. Whatever the reasons for needing to use the scheme, the effect is still the same: the loan does not appear in the balance sheet. Neither does the stock which has been sold. This may well be important if the company wants to demonstrate that it does not have a big stockholding problem or to show a more favourable return on assets.

In this respect, the scheme is similar to the consignment stock approach to off-balance-sheet finance in that neither the loan nor the assets to which it directly relates appear in the company's accounts. Again it will be a matter of interpretation when deciding how these schemes should be treated under FRS5. The scheme described above would be caught by the provisions of the standard. Accounting for a more complex scheme would require greater debate.

Still on the theme of using current assets to secure financing which does not have to be disclosed on the balance sheet as a loan is continued with the 'assignment of work-in-progress' scheme. This time, rather than an asset and the corresponding liability simply being excluded from the accounts the arrangement results in a reduction of the value which is attributed to the company's work in progress. It is a method of off-balance-sheet financing which is naturally most appropriate for those businesses which have long-term contracts which take some years to complete. The construction companies spring immediately to mind as potential users of this kind of scheme. Again the underlying reasons for adopting the scheme will be those related to short-term cash-flow shortages and already high gearing ratios.

Like the distillers which have to finance stock for several years before it can realize the investment which it ties up, the construction companies are also faced with the difficulty of financing a long-term project which will only produce cash some time after the necessary costs have been incurred. Again the spread of contracts and the timing of their completion would normally be expected to smooth out this lag in cash-flow receipts.

However, the construction industry has also found itself in difficulties on an international and national basis. The margins to be earned are barely noticeable and with competition intense, to say the least, the initiative remains very much with the giver of contract rather than the receiver. Front-end start-up costs are considerable and these have to be financed at a time when the banks remain dubious about increasing the levels of lending.

A further problem for the construction companies lies with the regular difficulties which they face during highly competitive times in obtaining progress payments on the contract. International contracts for developing companies tend to be the most problematic with a combination of administrative bureaucracy and balance of payments difficulties often leading to a delay in the cash being passed on to the construction company. It is to counter these cash-flow irregularities and at the same time keep the balance-sheet gearing in check that a company will adopt the assignment of work in progress approach to counter the problem.

The company will again deal through a bank or finance house. It agrees to assign irrevocably all the amounts which are payable under a major contract to the financier. At the same time the company also issues a bond which guarantees the performance of the contract which ensures that it is legally bound to complete the work. Having secured the assignment and the performance bond the finance house will then make periodic cash advances to the company. This will normally be in advance of work being carried out and allows the company to purchase the necessary materials and meet the other essential costs relating to the contract. Having made these advances the finance house also charges interest at a rate which will have been agreed as part of the deal.

This allows the construction company to carry out the contract without undue worry about the timing of progress payments from the client and without putting pressure on its other cash flow projections and the underlying strength, or weakness, of the balance sheet. Timing of payments cannot be ignored but the problems are less acute.

The scheme is devised in such a way that once the construction company has repaid the full amount of the cash advances, together with any interest which has accrued then, the balance outstanding under the contract is reassigned by the bank to the company. The arrangement therefore has considerable flexibility since the company can control the rate at which the advances are repaid. This might be at the same pace as the receipt of progress payments from the client or, if cash flow elsewhere in the business permits, at a quicker rate.

At the same time, the terms of assignment contract and the nature of the performance bond ensure that the company has no direct obligation to repay to the bank the amounts which it has advanced in order to finance the project. This meant that under the old regime there was no need for the company to disclose the advances in its accounts as a loan and the borrowing remained well and truly off balance sheet. The advances were treated simply as a reduction in the value of the company's work in progress in the same way that normal progress payments on account would be disclosed.

However, even under the old rules this type of transaction did not have complete immunity from disclosure requirements. The nature and terms of the performance bond dictate that a contingent liability is created and its existence must therefore be disclosed in the company's accounts by way of a note. That note can be vaguely drafted in such a way as not to reveal the full impact of the bond on the accounts and the company's off-balance-sheet financing activities, which allow it to reduce reported borrowings, remain a closely guarded secret. Using the substance over arguments of FRS5 the secrets may have to be shared a little more widely.

A more common form of off-balance-sheet financing is factoring. This is touched on in the chapter dealing with current assets and liabilities. It is a well-established technique which allows companies to obtain finance from sale of their customers' debts. The schemes are widely available and they do not have the stigma of some of the more complex techniques. However, there can be different forms of factoring which give rise to different treatments under FRS5. At the simplest level the debts are sold for a lump sum and that is the end of the matter. In this case the debts are no longer the asset of the seller. However, more complex arrangements can also be put in place which alter the dynamics of the transaction. At the opposite end of the spectrum the debts are little more than the collateral provided to a bank in return for the access to funds. Although there is a linkage it is borrowing by any other name and must be disclosed as such.

All four schemes which have so far been examined have been directly related to the company's assets. In many cases the underlying reason for using these off-balance-sheet financing methods will be simply to fund the assets to which the schemes relate. The more extreme factoring techniques are perhaps the only exception. Putting this aside it could therefore be argued that such schemes are merely practical solutions to commercial problems. Shareholders and users of accounts are not being deceived since the missing liability is matched by the missing asset although if an asset is 'sold' for an artificial profit then it will indeed be misleading. This argument does not, however, hold water when the funds are being raised to finance other projects or when commercial prudence would have dictated that the funds would not have been made available under straightforward borrowing arrangements. There is no doubt that off-balance-sheet financing, in whatever form, distorts the true state of a business but might also lead to misinformed business or investment decisions being taken by those who are obliged to rely on the accounts.

However, it must still be said that the schemes so far reviewed do generally have the feature, not in itself redeeming, of being linked to some real commercial aspect of the business. In this respect they differ wildly from some other schemes which are totally detached from any genuine transaction. These are little more than artificial devices to raise cash for the business without informing the outside world.

One scheme which might be described as borderline involves the sale and repurchase of property. Although these schemes again involve the use of the company's assets they tend to be constructed with the specific intention of raising funds.

These vary in sophistication. At the simplest level there is an old style sale and leaseback arrangement. A company sells its property to a third party and then agrees to lease it back. This is fairly straightforward in that the transaction is self-contained. The sale of the property is final. The company realizes capital funds but then has to pay rental to the new owner as it would with any leasehold agreement. This is a simple form of off-balance-sheet financing and sets out the basic principle of the schemes which are designed to secure funds but still allow the company to have use of the asset. The big difference is that while there is still an initial sale there is also an option to repurchase the asset in certain circumstances.

There are many variations on this basic theme and the ASB gives examples of how two might work in practice.

In the first a housebuilder, Company A, agrees to sell to a bank, Company B, some of the land contained within its holding. The arrangements surrounding the sale are as follows:

- The sales price will be the open market value as determined by an independent surveyor.
- The bank grants Company A the right to develop the land at any time during B's ownership, subject to its approval of the development plan. That approval will not be unreasonably withheld. For this right Company A pays all the outgoings on the land plus an annual fee of 5 per cent of the purchase price.
- The bank will maintain a memorandum account for the purpose of determining the price to be paid by Company A should it ever reacquire the land. In this account will be entered the original purchase price, any expenses incurred by the bank in relation to the transaction, a sum added quarterly (or on the sale by B of the land) calculated by reference to the bank's lending rate plus 2 per cent applied to the daily balance on the account. From the account will be deducted any annual fees paid by Company A to the bank.
- The bank grants Company A an option to acquire the land at any time within the next five years. The acquisition price is set at the balance on the memorandum account at the time of exercising the option.
- Company A grants the bank an option to require it to repurchase the land at any time within the next five years. The price will be the balance on the memorandum account at that time.

- On expiry of five years from the date of acquiring the land, the bank will offer it for sale generally. With the consent of Company A it may offer the land for sale at any time prior to that.
- In the event of the bank selling the land to a third party the proceeds of the sale shall be deducted from the memorandum account maintained by B. The balance on the account shall be settled between A and B as a retrospective adjustment of the price at which the bank originally purchased the land.

The advantages for Company A are clear. It releases a significant amount of capital in the short term yet still has the right to develop the land as it sees fit. For the bank's part it has secured a tidy bit of lending business. The loan is secured on the asset and it receives a commercial rate of return on its lending.

Under FRS5 this transaction would have to be disclosed as a secured loan since this is what is dictated by the commercial terms of the transaction. Company A continues to bear all the risks and rewards of ownership. It can still develop the land and bears all the resulting gains and losses. There is also an obligation to repay the whole of the sale proceeds initially received from the bank. Meanwhile the bank receives a lender's return and no more.

The second example of a sale and repurchase scheme is more complex. The basic transaction is the same in that Company A is selling part of its land holding. This time it makes use of a vehicle company V, which buys the land, and a subordinated loan to effect the transaction. The features of the agreement are as follows:

- The sale price is open market value.
- The bank grants the vehicle company V a loan of 60 per cent of the market value to effect the purchase. Company A provides V with a subordinated loan for the balance of the consideration. The bank's loan bears interest at 2 per cent above the base rate. Company A's loan bears interest at 10 per cent. All payments of interest and capital are subordinated to all sums due to the bank B in any period.

- Company V grants Company A the right to develop the land at any time during its ownership subject to approval. For this right Company A pays the vehicle company V a market rental on the land. If this is less than the interest which V has to pay on its loan from the bank then Company A will make up the shortfall as an addition to the subordinated loan.
- V grants A an option to acquire the land at any time within the next five years at a price equal to the sales price plus any incidental costs incurred by the vehicle company.
- On the expiry of 5 years from the date of acquiring the land the vehicle company will offer it for sale generally and may put it up for sale at any time before that with A's consent.
- In the event of V selling the land, the excess of the proceeds of sale and any other cash accumulated in the vehicle company over any sums due to the bank and company A under the terms of their respective loans will be paid immediately to A as a retrospective adjustment to the original purchase price.

The basic benefits and effects of the transaction are the same as those of the earlier, less complex transaction. Company A still continues to bear all the significant risk and rewards of the land bank. The vehicle company is protected against any losses and the bank merely secures a commercial return on its lending activities.

Hence FRS5 would demand that the liability be disclosed as a secured loan.

The standard also provides some further broad guidelines which will help decide how a sale and repurchase transaction should be treated. The aim here is to establish whether there has been a sale or not. Indications of a sale are as follows:

- No commitment for seller to repurchase the asset. There may be a call option but there would be a real possibility that it may not be exercised.
- Risk of changes in the asset value are borne by the buyer such that the buyer does not receive only a lender's return. This could be indicated by the sale and potential repurchase price being set at the prevailing market value.

- The nature of the asset is such that it will be used over the life of the agreement and the seller has no rights to determine its use. The seller has no rights to determine the asset's development or future sale.

Indications that there has been no sale and that the transaction should therefore be classified as a secured loan are as follows:

- The sale price does not equal market value at the date of sale.
- There is a commitment for the seller to repurchase the asset. There could for instance be put and call options with the same exercise price. Since the options give both the seller and the purchaser of the asset the right to enforce a resale at exactly the same price this would suggest that repurchase of the asset is bound to take place. Alternatively the seller may require the asset back to be used in its business or the asset is in effect the only source of the seller's future funds.
- The risk of changes to the asset value is borne by the seller such that the buyer receives only a lender's return. For example the repurchase price may equal the sales price plus costs and interest. Or the original purchase price may be adjusted retrospectively to pass variations in the value to the seller. Or the seller may provide residual value guarantees to the buyer or subordinated debt to protect the buyer from falls in the value of the asset.
- The seller retains the right to determine the asset's use, development or sale, or rights to profits therefrom.

Again these guidelines are helpful. But as we saw with consignment stock this check-list approach tends to detract from a standard which is relying for its strength on pursuing the broad principle of substance over form.

The implications for the standard are significant. If auditors are relying upon FRS5 to identify whether a scheme should be brought on the balance sheet or not then it will have considerable shortcomings. The argument in favour of this prescriptive approach is that it gives much more weight to the auditor who is struggling to persuade a client that an on-balance-sheet approach is needed. The difficulty is that very few of the schemes on the market will fit the description provided by the ASB. The biggest worry therefore is that each individual scheme will have to be tested in its own right. There is a means of doing this in the shape of the Urgent Issues Task Force. It has the power to rule on emerging and contentious questions. However, it was not set up to do the auditor's job for him. The last thing we need is a whole string of test cases. Apart from delay and frustration all it would do is create further uncertainty and provide just the rigid targets which the corporate financiers need in order to devise schemes to get around them.

This is going to be a particular problem in the most dangerous field of off-balance-sheet financing where the funding is secured through a separate specially constructed vehicle. The non-disclosed or quasi-subsidiary remains the most dangerous animal which the standard setters have to tame and of which investors should be distinctly wary.

These companies have all the attributes of a subsidiary in everything other than strict legal interpretation. Thankfully these artificial devices are less dangerous than they were before the 1989 Companies Act tightened up the rules on the legal definition of a subsidiary. Before those changes it was quite easy to construct a vehicle which, under the strictest legal interpretation, was not a subsidiary as defined in law. There were several ways of constructing this invisible subsidiary all of which are, by their very nature, quite complex, but with a little help from a company's financial advisers still surprisingly easy to implement.

Perhaps the most simple example of the non-disclosed subsidiary was that which involved a share capital which combined both ordinary shares and what were described as 'A' preference shares. Under company law both types of share are classified as equity capital, which was important for ensuring that the subsidiary remained off balance sheet. The ordinary and 'A' preference shares were issued in equal numbers. In order to make the scheme work, the holding company took into its ownership the ordinary shares which were issued. The parent's bankers then took up the 'A' preference shares.

Equal holding of the offshoot's share capital was insufficient to ensure that it would escape disclosure. The composition of the board of directors was equally important in deciding true ownership of a business. Therefore, in setting up the subsidiary its articles were constructed in such a way that ensures that the holding company and the bank had the right to appoint an equal number of directors, although there were often means by which the company had more votes than the bank.

The decision, under the pre-1989 legislation, as to whether a company was a subsidiary rested on the answer to two simple questions. Does the holding company own more than 50 per cent of the equity share capital and does it control composition of the board of directors? If either question was answered in the affirmative then the new company was deemed to be a subsidiary. Clearly, though, by using the method outlined above the answer to both questions was negative. A company with the structure described above avoided consolidation and therefore stayed off balance sheet.

This was a clear problem and the 1989 Companies Act went a long way to tightening up the legislation. Its requirements focus much more on voting rights than equity control. An undertaking will be deemed to be the parent of a subsidiary undertaking where any of the following applies:

- It holds a majority of the voting rights.
- It is a member and has the right to appoint or remove directors holding a majority of the voting rights at meetings of the board or on all or substantially all matters.
- It has the right to exercise a dominant influence over the undertaking by virtue of provisions contained in the memorandum or articles of association or by virtue of a control contract.
- It is a member of the undertaking and controls alone, following an agreement with other shareholders, a majority of the voting rights.

– It has a participating interest in the undertaking and actually exercises a dominant influence over the undertaking or it and the undertaking are managed on a unified basis.

This changes the entire thrust of the legislation and has rendered many of the old vehicles redundant by bringing them on balance sheet. However, it has not stamped out the quasi-subsidiary entirely and it is still possible to construct vehicles which escape the legal definition. There have been a pro-liferation, for instance, of joint venture companies which put the subsidiary definition to the test.

The quasi-subsidiary is addressed by FRS5. It says that attention should be focused on the benefits arising from the net assets of the vehicle being examined. Evidence of who gets the benefits will be found by which party is exposed to the risks inherent in those assets. In determining whether a parent controls a vehicle regard should be given to who, in practice, directs the financial and operating policies of the vehicle. The ability to prevent others from directing the policies is evidence of control as is the ability to prevent others from enjoying the benefits arising from the vehicle's net assets. Sometimes those policies will be predetermined in which case the party having control is the one which enjoys the benefits arising from the net assets.

The combination of FRS5 and the tighter Companies Act makes life more difficult for the creative accountant. However, the quasi-subsidiary will no doubt continue to thrive. The ASB is trying to offset some of the problems which might be encountered by tightening up on the treatment of associate and joint venture companies. A discussion document proposes making the definition of an associated company more restrictive and suggests expanding the definition of a joint venture. Improved disclosure and the requirement to reflect the results of joint ventures in the group profit and loss account has been mooted.

It is certainly an area which will demand constant attention. As long as the rules exist which allow two companies involved in a joint venture which rids them of a troublesome aspect of their business and which is not reflected in either set of accounts, then there are difficulties.

The problem for the standard setters is that having set their stall out the corporate financiers now have all they need to begin devising schemes which get around the rules. The disclosure of the substance rather than the form of a vehicle requires a tremendous amount of good will on the part of the preparer. If that is not forthcoming and if the auditing profession is prepared to support the principle only timidly then the difficulties will not go away.

So far we have dealt with specific schemes and devices which demand a degree of sophistication. There is an altogether more crude form of off-balance-sheet financing which in essence involves ignoring a liability altogether. Most notable here is the question of deferred consideration which was particularly widespread among the service industries. It is quite an effective weapon in that a company is acquired but only part of the payment is made at the outset. The balance falls due some time later. The concept of the earn out was particularly appealing in the so-called people businesses. The assets of the business being acquired were essentially the key staff with their expertise and client relationships who also often owned the business. The business would be worth much less if key people left so the earn out acted as incentive for them to stay. It was designed to maximize their performance and that of the business which had been acquired. A good performance would bring significant further payments two or three years after the acquisition.

The acquiring company had the full benefit of the business which had been bought but was not recognizing the full extent of the liability. Ultimately these deferred payments caused significant problems particularly for one or two of the big advertising agencies.

If these unrecognized liabilities exist they will often be identified in the contingent liability notes which should be one of the most avidly read elements of any set of accounts. The contingency may never crystallize but when it does it can often come roaring back on to the balance sheet with devastating consequences.

The main problem with off-balance-sheet financing in general and with the quasi-subsidiary method in particular is that it threatens to distort the truth and fairness of the accounts. While there is no legal requirement for companies to report these schemes in their accounts the chances of creative accounting becoming deceptive accounting are greatly increased. Shareholders and other users of the accounts are making decisions under a cloud of uncertainty using information which may be neither full nor fair. A group which according to its published balance sheet may have little or no borrowings could in fact be riddled with debt which has been arranged off balance sheet. The great problem is that it can, even with improved disclosure and tightened rules, still be difficult to assess the real implications of these schemes. The complex nature of the transactions and the way in which they are implemented may make control difficult but this is not a reason in itself to ignore the problem. The underlying reason for off-balance-sheet financing is to present the company's financial position in a different and more favourable light. The arguments to justify off-balance-sheet financing are similar to those used to support the publishing and sale of pornography in that it fulfils a genuine corporate need and therefore is a service to society. To legislate too strongly against it would only drive it underground and make it even more difficult to control.

The final view you take on off-balance-sheet financing may well depend on your views on pornography.

11. Acquisitions and Mergers

Acquisitions and mergers will always have a special place in the annals of accounting history. If creative accounting is the golden egg then it was acquisition and merger accounting which came close to strangling the goose which laid it. It was the consequences of excessive abuses in this area which lay behind many of the exotic corporate collapses. It was those collapses which focused attention so sharply on the quality of financial reporting.

In the end the history of acquisition accounting has a profile which is perhaps not dissimilar to that of drug addiction. Here was a new idea which the trendiest of corporate finance pushers were offering to their clients. It was fine they said, it was perfectly safe they said, no harm would come of it they said and it would provide the business with a real buzz. Sure enough it was as they said. But this recreational creative accounting gave way to something altogether more sinister. Little acquisitions became bigger acquisitions. Rules which had been tweaked were aggressively bent. And the corporate high which could be attained was awesome.

Sometimes, often without realizing it, companies became addicted. But now the drug was coursing through its veins to an extent that both the company and the pushers were feeding off each other's frenzy. It was no longer possible just to make one acquisition. Each demanded another, even bigger than the one before, to satisfy the needs of the company and more importantly those of an impressed and intrigued audience which was unaware that the tremendous earnings energy was a product of this gnawing addiction.

To these companies reality was little more than an illusion brought about by a lack of acquisitions.

As with any form of addiction those who were unaware of their problem found that they had lost control. Whether it was acquisition overdose or misjudgements caused by the numbing effects of the drug or simply fatigue the habit began to get the better of them. One by one they began to break up.

In some cases it was possible to identify other reasons why corporate collapses occurred but a common strand was that the companies involved were inevitably aggressive and acquisitive businesses.

The onlookers who had been once so admiring began to question why it was that the addiction had not manifested itself earlier. To that extent they began to examine more closely the role of financial accounts in the process. What they discovered was not to their liking and as we have already seen it created both an impetus and an environment for the quality of financial reporting to be improved.

It is testimony to the ASB's commitment to securing a sustainable improvement in quality that it was not rushed into securing a hasty solution to this thorny problem. For while many abuses were carried out in the name of mergers and acquisition accounting there was little point in merely trying to close loopholes. The experience of the old regime dictated that new ones would be opened before the old ones were closed. Although this is an area which has clearly been on the ASB's agenda from the outset it has taken a more considered approach. This is entirely appropriate since mergers and acquisitions cannot be treated in isolation and have to be examined in the overall context of the new regime which is being created and alongside important but related issues such as goodwill.

Now at last the ASB has produced a new standard and it threatens to be the most controversial set of rules yet published. It brings the ASB into direct conflict with both preparers and auditors of accounts and the success it has in securing compliance will be a crucial test of the tone which will be set for standard setters for the rest of the millennium.

The reform of acquisition accounting has been developed on a range of fronts but by far the biggest source of disquiet is the proposal to bar companies from setting up fair value provisions in respect of restructuring and reorganization costs. This has been one of the richest seams for the creative accountant to mine. It has allowed companies effectively to ring fence the profit and loss from the financial implications of restructuring the acquired company and in some cases the combined group.

It has become the hallmark of the acquisitive company that its balance sheet is littered with provisions, often of substance, and normally dominated by those arising on acquisition. The most often referred to example is Hanson which in its 1993 accounts boasted of provisions for liabilities and charges of £5.8 billion. Of this £2.3 billion related to pensions and employee obligations, £1.4 billion related to reclamation and environmental obligations, £600 million related to taxation and £1.5 billion was classified as 'other'.

The note gives some further amplification of these provisions. The pensions provision includes £1,067 million for payments into coal-industry-funded trusts to meet health and welfare costs of miners who retired from the industry prior to 1976 and for those receiving black lung benefits. These payments will be made over thirty years. Provisions for reclamation include £128 million for production-based payments to be made over the next twelve years to a coal-industry-funded trust. The environmental provisions included £849 million relating to Beazer's former US chemical operations disposed of by Beazer prior to its acquisition by Hanson. Beazer and certain of its subsidiaries remain contractually and statutorily liable for certain environmental costs relating to these discontinued operations. These and other costs are payable over periods of up to thirty years. The mysteriously named 'other provisions' relate to insurance, legal and financing matters and costs relating to acquisitions, disposals and rationalizations both established on acquisitions and provided for in current and prior years.

The provisions are by any measure significant and as can be seen quite broad ranging. The £5.8 billion total must be seen in the context of the group's capital and reserves of just £3.9 billion. However, their more important implications are for the profit and loss account. By taking these provisions up front, on acquisition, Hanson is effectively restricting the subsequent charges to the profit and loss account. The 1,067 provision to meet health and welfare costs for miners relates to payments spread over thirty years. Hanson could quite conceivably charge £35 million a year against reported profits. However, because the provision has already been set up the charge is dealt with instead through the balance sheet. The profit and loss account is protected. The approach is entirely acceptable but does bring advantages for the company.

To gauge some idea of the overall impact it is worth comparing the provisions utilized during the year with those created. This ignores those created on acquisition. In the 1993 accounts Hanson spells out quite clearly that a total of £199 million of provisions were made in the year while £530 million were utilized. The net benefit is therefore £331 million. It is only a rough guide but it gives some impression of the scale of the issue particularly in the context of the company which made pre-tax profits of £1,103 billion in the year.

This approach is entirely consistent with the old rules and importantly the disclosure is very good. Investors prepared to venture into the notes to the accounts can assess quite easily the extent of the provisions. However, the ASB was rightly concerned that this is an area which is too open to abuse. Indeed it was the ability of companies to flatter their earnings while weakening their balance sheets which was at the root of some of the corporate disasters of the late eighties and early nineties.

The legitimacy of these provisions came from the rules on acquisition accounting which obliged companies to attribute a fair value to the assets and liabilities of the businesses they acquired. The difference between this figure and that actual consideration was deemed to be goodwill and as the chapter dealing with intangible assets shows it can be treated in any number of ways. Often the goodwill is written off directly to reserves.

However, the fair value exercise allowed companies to reflect changes they planned to make to the acquired businesses. It was in this grey area that many of the abuses began and some quite liberal interpretations were applied. Some companies made provisions for restructuring not just the acquired business but also existing businesses within the group. Similarly provisions for losses on businesses that were to be disposed of were extended to those losses incurred by continuing businesses.

These techniques were clearly unacceptable and there was widespread agreement that reform was required. What was not anticipated, however, was quite how radical that reform would be. Few had imagined that the ASB would go so far as to outlaw these provisions altogether.

The essence of the ASB's thinking is that the assets and liabilities recognized in the allocation of fair value should be those of the acquired business at the date of acquisition. They should not be increased or decreased by changes that result from the acquirer's intention to take action in the future. The ASB insists that the fair values attributed to liabilities should not include provisions for future operating losses or for reorganization and integration costs which are expected to be incurred as a result of the acquisition. These losses and costs must instead be reported as part of the post-acquisition financial performance of the acquiring group.

The rules also address other issues such as the fair value of non-monetary assets which must be measured at the market value or if there is no proper and accessible market at lower than replacement cost and recoverable amount. The fair value should reflect the condition of the assets at the time of acquisition but not any impairment resulting from subsequent events.

The rules set out the application of the proposed principles to determining fair values for particular categories of assets and liabilities but the overriding thrust is to make a clear distinction between the fair value at the date of acquisition and what those values might be once the impact of any future actions is taken into consideration.

This is much to the liking of users of accounts and rightly so. The fair value provisions represent a significant opportunity to distort the underlying profitability of a business. As such any move to outlaw them must be welcomed.

However, it has not been welcomed at all by preparers and by some auditors. This is largely because they see a gaping loophole being swiftly tightened. They can also marshal some superficially attractive arguments why some element of provisioning should be legitimately classified as part of the effective cost of the acquisition.

One worry expressed is that because the rules are regarded as being inappropriate and misfounded by many preparers it may well encourage a concerted effort to bend the rules. Some loopholes have already been identified. There is, for instance, the potential for collusion between the acquiring company and its target to ensure that reorganization costs and asset write-downs are made in the pre-acquisition period. The same kinds of problem could arise in the context of business disposals where some pre-acquisition tinkering could be implemented. These are discussed in more detail later in the chapter.

Another difficulty is that if companies are so committed to the concept of making provisions for future reorganizations then they could still do so. Those provisions could not be masked as part of the cost of acquisition but they could still be made and disclosed as an exceptional item. In theory this should count against earnings for the year. But as the chapter on presentation indicates there is a high degree of uncertainty over whether the all-embracing earnings figures has any relevance. While investors pay more attention to headline earnings excluding exceptional items the company will still be able to achieve its objective of setting up the provisions without its earnings profile being penalized. Once the provisions are established they can then be used to protect the profit and loss account in subsequent years. The argument then is that the problem is not being solved; it is simply being moved to another part of the accounts.

It is a genuine concern. However, the abuse will only work as long as investors and users are prepared to overlook this clumsy sleight of hand. There has been some concern expressed by investors about provisioning generally and it is therefore within their gift to do something about it. If they are happy for companies to remove slabs of costs from the continuing profit and loss account and expose themselves to a severe misunderstanding of a company's position then so be it. If not then they should take a more rigorous line with companies which continue to counter the spirit if not the letter of the new rules.

These are practical arguments against the ASB's thinking although they are founded in a lack of conviction that users will comply with the spirit of the standard. They are therefore weaker than the arguments which deal with the logic which underpins the ASB's assumption. The rules imply that no account should be taken of management's intentions at the time of acquisition. This is an understandable response to the historical flimsiness of management intentions. It therefore overlooks the fact that the very nature of some acquisitions quite clearly indicates that restructuring will take place. If for instance a company takes over a business which is in financial difficulties and where its viability is threatened then only the most stupid of managements would take it on and run it in exactly the same way. Changes are bound to follow since rarely is one company going to buy another simply to allow it to go bust. By the same token there are occasions when specific intentions are set out and must be regarded as an essential part of the acquisition. This was highlighted by the take-over bid for William Low, the Scottish supermarket chain, in 1994. Both Tesco and Sainsbury launched competing bids. What they both had in common was that they both said that they would close down Low's Scottish headquarters in Dundee. Neither

Sainsbury nor Tesco needed the headquarters and indeed closure was an integral part of the sums done in order to justify the price which was being paid. The closure costs therefore became very much part of the acquisition process yet under the new rules no provision could be reflected in the fair values attributed to the Low assets.

The difficulty for the ASB is that it is hard to find a reliable halfway house. Once it strays from a hard and fast rule, then in creeps flexibility and scope for creative interpretation of the rules. Management intention has been notoriously imprecise in the past. There is no reason why it should get any clearer in the future.

No doubt some preparers and auditors would have preferred an approach which involved drafting rules which dealt with the obvious abuses which arose because of the defects in the old regime. These tended to relate to the blurred distinction between the acquired business and the existing business. With greater clarity in this area together with more rigid application of disclosure requirements relating to the reorganization provisions, their timing and the cash flow implications then it is argued the ASB's aims could have been achieved without alienating a large proportion of preparers.

The problem now is that a standard is on the books which does not inspire confidence and which some regard as defective. These are the circumstances which encourage creativity. The potential abuses which have already been identified could become more actively pursued. This could have the most unfortunate effect of pushing the implications of these abuses more deeply underground where it will be difficult for investors to assess the consequences.

On the question of collusion between the acquiring company and the target the rules do not readily identify the circumstances where provisions and write-downs take place in advance of the take-over. There are two problems here. First companies will still have the considerable benefit of the provisions which are established but more worrying is that the costs will be hidden in the analysis of the book value of assets and liabilities rather than highlighted as a fair value adjustment or post-acquisition charge. The ASB suggest that where there is a suspicion of collusion the auditors should assess whether control passed at an earlier date presumably at the point the provisions are created. This is unlikely to prove an adequate counter to the problem since the making of the provisions will be a prerequisite of the deal going ahead rather than a direct order from the acquiring company. This could prove to be a significant loophole. It will not be applicable to hostile take-over but as many more deals are agreed rather than contested these days it will remain a fruitful area for those who want to bend the rules. The ASB has certainly attempted to limit the scope for abuse, for instance by requiring disclosure of provisions made by an acquired company in the twelve months prior to acquisition, but there is still a way to exploit the rules for those who have the will.

Another potential area for abuse lies in the inconsistency between the rules on closing a business and selling a business. The fair value of non-monetary assets should be the lower of replacement cost and recoverable amount. If the decision is taken to close an operation the acquirer is not allowed to reflect assets at realizable value because the decision will be deemed to be a subsequent event. In contrast to this if the acquirer decides to sell an operation it should be valued at net realizable value.

It can be reasonably assumed that where a business is to be sold the provisions required to reduce the business to net realizable value would include the costs of any redundancies, reorganizations or stock write-downs that were required to bring the business to a saleable state. Providing these provisions were justified as slimming down or tidying up exercises rather than material change then they would be allowed. These provisions would not be permitted if a business were being closed down. There is therefore a temptation for companies to seek to identify businesses as being held for resale rather than closure. It is not at all difficult to put an advertisement in the newspapers offering it for sale. The rules merely require that a business be separately identifiable, that a buyer is being sought and that the sale is reasonably expected to occur within a year. The treatment would have to be reversed if the sale did not ultimately occur but there is a degree of flexibility which could be exploited.

The advantage is clear. By identifying a business as for sale the rules can be circumvented and the provisions which the ASB is seeking to outlaw will still be made as part of the fair value process.

As we have already seen there is the potential for abuse through collusion between the acquiring company and the target over the timing of pre-acquisition provisions. Although such collusion is not available in contested take-overs this does not necessarily restrict creativity when a company has been acquired through a hostile bid. It will often be the case that the accounts of the target company will be prepared by the management of the new owners for both the pre- and post-acquisition periods. In these circumstances it will be possible for reorganization and redundancy costs to be pushed into the pre-acquisition period and dealt with as part of the fair value process rather than carried forward and taken as a charge against profits in the post-acquisition period. The argument could be made that the provisions should have been created by the old management even if they had not flagged their intention to so do. It would be hard to make this work since FRS7 requires a commitment to exist before acquisition and the acquirer would need to show that the assets of the target were impaired at the date of the take-over. However, subjectivity is again creeping into the equation.

Already then it is possible to see that a standard which starts out with the best intentions is in danger of being undermined. It could become a victim of its own success. All the more reason then for investors to be aware of the benefits for them of the ASB's ruling and support it more forcefully than they have in the past.

Without this the question of excessive provisions on acquisition will at best be diverted to another part of the accounts and at worst pushed even further underground. Whether the position will be altered by any move the ASB makes to establish a framework for the treatment of goodwill remains to be seen.

Increased goodwill is a natural counter to increased provisions. What those provisions do is reduce the net assets of the acquired business, therefore increasing the gap between these and the actual price paid. That gap is filled by goodwill. The lower the net assets the higher the goodwill. As Sir David Tweedie has pointed out, in the three years after the introduction of the original standard dealing with acquisition accounting the level of goodwill as a proportion of purchase cost rose from 11 per cent to 44 per cent. It can be assumed that this was in part due to a decline in net assets brought about by the creation of provisions.

When goodwill is written off it depletes the balance sheet although those companies which have been able to argue that purchased goodwill is in part attributable to the value of acquired brands have discovered a way to secure protection for the profit and loss account while keeping the value of the balance sheet strong. However, a workable solution to the goodwill problem looks further away than ever before and it is hard to see how this might provide a spur to the curtailment of provisions.

Ironically one of the simplest ways of dealing with goodwill has itself been virtually outlawed by the ASB. In a separate but clearly related exposure draft to that dealing with fair values the ASB has proposed that merger accounting, where goodwill does not arise at all, is restricted to very limited circumstances.

Under acquisition accounting fair values must be established with the balance between net assets and the purchase price treated as goodwill. Using merger accounting, however, the two businesses are combined on an equal footing normally without any requirement to restate net assets to fair value. Rather than include the results of the acquired company from the date of acquisition with merger accounting the results for both companies are included for the whole of the accounting period including the time before the merger took place. In other words a merger could take place on 31 December but the results for that year would be presented on the basis that the merger had taken place twelve months earlier on 1 January. That has its attractions but more significantly the shares which are used as consideration are recorded at their nominal value. The differences which arise on consolidation are that much smaller but are not treated as goodwill, being deducted instead from reserves.

There was some attraction for companies in not creating goodwill and the prospect of securing 365 days of profit for just 1 day of merger was also appealing. However, the interest in merger accounting waned considerably once companies latched on to the even richer pickings which lay in acquisition accounting and in particular through fair value provisions.

Fearing that the crack-down on these provisions would lure companies back to merger accounting the ASB has therefore tightened the rules. In future acquisition accounting will have to be used for all business combinations where a party can be identified as having the role of an acquirer. Merger accounting will be restricted to those business combinations where acquisition accounting would not properly reflect the true nature of the combination. A merger is defined as being a business combination in which, rather than one party acquiring control of another, the parties come together to share in the future risks and benefits of the combined entity. It will not be the augmentation of one company by the addition of another but the creation of a new reporting entity.

The ASB has set out five criteria which must be met before merger accounting can he used. These relate to:

- the way the roles of each party to the combination are portrayed;
- the involvement of each party to the combination in the selection of the management of the combined entity;
- the relative sizes of the parties;

- whether shareholders of the combining entities receive any consideration other than equity shares in the combined entity;
- whether shareholders of the combining entities retain an interest in the performance of part only of the combined entity.

The aim is clearly to drive companies away from merger accounting and herd them back towards acquisition accounting. That is a laudable objective providing the acquisition rules are secure and, as we have seen, there must be some doubts about that.

The real test of the rules will come when merger and acquisition activity is at a higher level than during recessionary times. The dynamics of a business change and the pressures on the finance director to explore different accounting avenues intensifies. The difficulties with this area are not going to go away and it will remain one of the most contentious accounting areas simply because the stakes can be extremely high.

The bigger worry from the overall standard setting perspective is that the rules will set the ASB too much in conflict with industry. A little tension can be creative but if this turns to outright confrontation then some quite fundamental structural problems are created. That confrontation will be defused providing the big institutional investors rally quite firmly behind the ASB. It is very much in their interests that companies do not ring fence their profit and loss account. As the prime beneficiaries of the new rules it is incumbent upon them to lend the support the ASB needs.

12. Brands and Goodwill

It is hard enough to construct rules dealing with items which physically exist. Imagine then the problems which arise when an attempt is made to attribute valuations to things which cannot be seen or touched. Unsurprisingly this is an area which has been the subject of much debate but not a great deal of specific action.

The treatment of these intangible assets is particularly complex because of the range of items which fall into the classification. At the heart of the uncertainty is goodwill, an area which has vexed the profession for years. But compounding that uncertainty is the valuation attributable to internally generated intangibles such as trademarks, patents and brands.

That starting point for the problem is the accountancy profession's preoccupation with double-entry bookkeeping. The principle that for every debit there must be a credit has been an essential part of the process for centuries. It worked very well until the age of the acquisition which threw up an anomaly which threatened this most basic of basic principles. In order to secure a business the bidding company will often offer a premium for control. The total purchase price therefore exceeds the value of the underlying net assets.

This represents a nightmare for the double entry bookkeeping control freak. If a business with net assets of £10 million is bought for £20 million what happens to the difference of £10 million? The answer comes in the shape of goodwill. It provides a neat theoretical justification for the discrepancy in that goodwill represents the intangible value generated by a business above and beyond its asset base. It can be explained by a particularly loyal customer base or a reputation for service, a dominant market position or a whole range of intellectual justifications. More importantly it also squares the double-entry circle paving the way as it does for the equal and opposite matching of debits with credits.

In essence goodwill is an artificial device created for the convenience of the bookkeeper. As Baron Frankenstein discovered with his artificial creation messing about with nature can sometimes have unfortunate consequences. Goodwill is yet to be the ruin of the standard setters but there is no doubt that the villagers remain a little restless.

The problem for the accountants is that having created this monster it has grown and grown to an extent where it has become almost impossible to tame without inflicting great pain. Goodwill may have appeared like a good idea at the time it was invented but the creators did not envisage the scale of the take-overs and the size of the control premiums which would be paid for businesses in the eighties and nineties.

It is testimony to the size of the problem that when the Accounting Standards Board launched its discussion paper on the question of goodwill in December 1993 it was not exactly brimming with confidence about finding a solution.

The ASB recognized that purchased goodwill is an accounting anomaly and that there is no complete solution to the question of the appropriate accounting treatment for it. Sir David Tweedie admitted that there was no obvious solution waiting to be adopted. As if to confirm the extent of the dilemma it emerged that the ASB members were split down the middle on whether goodwill should be written off immediately to reserves or whether it should be capitalized and depreciated over a period of time.

The debate on how to deal with the problem has to be conducted at two levels. First there is the question of how to deal with purchased goodwill which is effectively an accounting mechanism used to sort out the difference between the purchase price of a business and its net asset value. The second element of the equation is how to reconcile the treatment of purchased goodwill with that afforded to internally generated goodwill which has not been bought in but which a company's management feels ought to be recognized in its accounts.

It is an issue which is particularly pertinent in the context of brands which as any marketing man worth his salt will tell you are of immense importance to a business. In its 1993 accounts Guinness states quite unequivocally: 'Brands represent the Group's most valuable asset.'

Other companies would agree entirely with this assertion and indeed many consumer goods companies now reflect a value for their brands in the balance sheet.

In Guinness's case the company takes account of its acquired brands only when they have a substantial and long-term value, title is clear, brand earnings are separately identifiable, the brand could be sold separately from the rest of the business and where the brand achieves earnings in excess of unbranded products. This is a not untypical approach. However, what it effectively does is to describe goodwill as intangible assets.

In Guinness's case its 1993 balance sheet included a value of £2,154 million as the cost of its acquired brands. Grand Metropolitan in its 1993 accounts included a valuation of £2,924 million for its acquired brands again described as intangible assets.

Both companies assess the values of these brands annually and both conclude that the brands are worth more than the value at which they are recorded in the accounts.

Ironically, in the case of Guinness, its most famous brand is the eponymous stout yet despite its clear value to the company no account is taken of it. Others have not been so conservative and RHM, in its days of independence, actually placed a value on its internally generated brands.

The ASB has tried to cut through the distinction between purchased intangible assets and those which are internally generated by denying the existence of the former. In its discussion document it argues that there should be no separate treatment for purchased intangible assets which ought instead to be subsumed within purchased goodwill and accounted for accordingly.

Conc

This is dangerous territory since it merely puts the whole question of intangible assets, be they brands or customer lists, to one side. The potential for inconsistency is considerable in that the ASB is seeking a solution for goodwill yet not dealing with one of its key components. This is particularly frustrating given that the ASB is not clear in its own mind how to deal with goodwill.

The discussion paper offers a number of potential treatments. Three are asset-based methods and three involve elimination. The first of the asset-based methods involves purchased goodwill being capitalized and then amortized over a predetermined finite life subject to a maximum of perhaps twenty years. The amortized carrying value would be reviewed each year. The second method would again involve capitalization but it would then be amortized through a systematic annual review procedure to estimate the required annual charge which in some years could be zero. The third method, in true old style standard setting speak, would involve a combination of the previous two methods. The first would be used for most acquisitions but the second could be used in limited special circumstances where the goodwill is thought to have an economic life greater than twenty years. Those special circumstances are described by the ASB in terms which are not exactly fighting for selection in any awards for plain English. It says:

> The special and limited circumstances where capitalization and annual review would be appropriate are those where it is impossible to make with any reasonable degree of precision a determination of the useful economic life of the goodwill beyond an assessment, on the basis of all relevant factors (including the historical experience of the economic life of goodwill of a similar nature both in the business in question and generally), that the goodwill concerned has a useful economic life of more than twenty years.

The great irony is that it is this third compromise and unclear method which had the most appeal for ASB members supportive of the asset based options. It represents a virtual admission that as far as goodwill is concerned then anything goes.

Turning to the elimination methods which the ASB puts forward there are again three options. The first is for purchased goodwill to be eliminated against reserves immediately on acquisition. The second is for the goodwill to be transferred, immediately on acquisition, to a separate goodwill write-off reserve. The third option is again for a transfer to a separate goodwill write-off reserve with the balance contained in this reserve assessed each year for recoverability. Any adjustment resulting from this exercise would be taken as a charge against the profit and loss account.

Of the elimination methods proposed there was support but again no majority for the second option. This is not surprising in that the goodwill is being transferred rather than eliminated which again takes you into the area of compromise which is so popular with the standard setters when dealing with goodwill.

It is apparent then that there is no obvious solution beckoning. The ASB has already hinted through the preferred options indicated by its members that the lines of least resistance and therefore greatest compromise offer the greatest attraction. Unfortunately compromise has not fathered too many effective standards. The danger for the ASB is if it forces itself into making a decision then that decision will either be flawed or will be so insubstantial that the rules will be rendered immediately ineffective. That would be damaging not just for the standards in question but also for the integrity of the standard setting process.

The other problem which the ASB faces is that it is in danger of heading towards confrontation with the corporate sector. Company executives do not take kindly to the suggestion that they ought to reduce either their profits for the year or the value of their balance sheet or both. If Guinness had been obliged to write off the value of its brands, for which read purchased goodwill, over twenty years its profits each year would be reduced by over £100 million. In 1993 that would have been equivalent to a reduction of around 15 per cent in reported pre-tax profits. Retained earnings would have been slashed by over half. A complete write-off would slash the Guinness net asset value by over half.

These are not strong selling points for any kind of radical solution to the goodwill/intangible asset problem. But while it remains unresolved it merely creates further opportunity for distortion and manipulation. It also makes it more difficult for the ASB to move towards a solution for related issues. The whole purchased goodwill question is wrapped up with the question of accounting for acquisitions which is itself an area of not inconsiderable controversy. The rules on acquisitions are bound to have an impact on the purchased goodwill since it is by definition the difference between the purchase price and the underlying net assets.

The acquisitions issue is dealt with in a separate chapter but the purchased goodwill problem also has implications for the treatment of internally generated goodwill. It is very hard to have a set of rules dealing with goodwill which is brought in while ignoring that which the company creates of its own accord. Put in simple terms why should Guinness stout only acquire a monetary value which can be reflected in the balance sheet when it is acquired by somebody else. It is a powerful brand yet the company has chosen, prudently, not to incorporate its value in the accounts.

Other companies have taken a more aggressive attitude to their home-grown brands and attributed some kind of value to their intangible assets. This is an altogether more complex question and one which offers tremendous scope for the creative accountant. These intangible assets can be quite widespread in their nature. Some will be more easily quantifiable than others and may even have their basis in an established cost. For most, however, the very fact that the assets are intangible means that a range of quite subjective judgements will need to be made. Whenever opinion has greater influence than fact the prospects for creativity are increased considerably.

Perhaps the most pertinent area to consider in detail, however, is that of home-grown brands. This is where the debate has been most heated and where there is an established inconsistency of treatment with acquired brands.

The best illustration of the problems comes through an analysis of Rank Hovis McDougall which pioneered the concept of putting brands on to the balance sheet. It not only offers an insight into the techniques which underpin the valuation process but also highlights some of the pitfalls. As the company was taken over by Tomkins in 1992 it more interestingly allows consideration of the issue in the context of the ultimate test of an independent outside valuation.

RHM is a food manufacturer owning some of Britain's best-known brands including Hovis, Mother's Pride, Golden Shred marmalade, Paxo stuffing, Saxa salt, Bisto gravymaker, McDougall's flour and Mr Kipling cakes. In the eighties the company was performing well and between 1983 and 1987 increased its pre-tax profits from £44.1 million to £116.1 million. At that point the company took no account of the value of its brands although their importance was recognized. The 1987 annual report records that success in food manufacturing is not a short-term phenomenon and points out that the reputation of the brands has been built up over a number of years supported by significant spending on advertising and by the company's marketing expertise.

However, alongside the development of the business there was also an intriguing sub-plot provided by the presence on RHM's share register of Goodman Fielder Wattie, the Australasian food company, which had built a near 30 per cent holding in the company. Its presence was clearly regarded as something of a threat. The concerns that it may be a prelude to a take-over were increased by the general fascination at that time with brands. They had become very much the flavour of the month particularly in the food sector. At every turn it seemed that there was a bidder prepared to pay a healthy premium for control of consumer brands. A number of food manufacturing companies changed hands not always in friendly circumstances and often at fancy prices. The most notable take-over bid was for Rowntree, the famous chocolate manufacturer, which was ultimately devoured by Nestlé of Switzerland. The exit multiple was twenty-six times historic earnings but some food companies were sold on an historic multiple of thirty-five times earnings. It was apparent that brands were attractive and that they could command bid premiums which were not reflected in the stock market's valuation of the company controlling these household names.

It was against this backdrop that in 1988 Goodman Fielder Wattie duly launched a take-over for RHM. The 465p a share bid valued the company as a whole at around £1.7 billion. It was fiercely resisted and one of the main planks of the RHM defence was that the bid failed to recognize the value of the company's brands.

In one of its defence documents the company said: 'RHM owns a number of strong brands, many of which are market leaders, which are valuable in their own right, but which the stock market tends consistently to undervalue. These valuable assets are not included in RHM's balance sheet, but they have helped RHM build profits in the past and provide a sound base for future growth.'

It pointed to a number of factors to justify its arguments. Brand advertising in the five years to 1987 had amounted to £98 million. Even a commodity product like salt had benefited from the Saxa brand name which led to margin benefits. Bisto had been a dominant brand for seventy-eight years. Mr Kipling which had been started in 1967 had secured a 36 per cent share of the branded packaged cake market and achieved annual sales of nearly £100 million by 1987.

This was just the kind of robust material which makes for a good take-over battle. In the end, however, shareholders did not have to decide on the outcome of the bid since it was referred to the Monopolies and Mergers Commission and Goodman Fielder Wattie decided not to pursue the offer.

The effect of the bid was to jerk RHM into accounting action. The bid may have lapsed but Goodman still owned a near 30 per cent stake in RHM which would provide a powerful platform from which another bid could be launched. The company was determined that its brands should no longer go unrecognized. In its 1988 accounts the company therefore decided to include a valuation for all its brands either acquired or home grown.

At a stroke the balance sheet was transformed. A business which had boasted fixed assets of £425.7 million in 1987 could now lay claim to a total of £1,142.4 million, courtesy of the £678 million injection of the brands as intangible assets. The total net assets of £265.2 million in 1987 had almost quadrupled to £978.7 million. What is more the company went to great lengths to point out that this was a conservative valuation. The £678 million attributed to brands was not an estimate of their worth in the open market. Far from being a price tag it was merely an assessment of the current value of the brands to the group. The figure excluded any tangible assets and made no allowance for other associated intangibles such as management, the workforce or technical expertise.

The move created a storm of controversy and did not exactly meet with universal approval. This was not surprising given that RHM was the first company to attempt the exercise. However, there was nothing that stood in RHM's way. The auditors gave the treatment a clean bill of health and the standard setters were not in any position to argue formally against it.

The treatment remained unchallenged until RHM was taken over, and while it did not lead to a deluge of copycat approaches there were occasional examples of internally generated brands being brought on to balance sheets. More importantly it raised the level of debate about brands and indirectly goodwill. That remains pertinent to the questions the ASB faces today.

The arguments in favour of capitalization of brands have not changed a great deal and while valuation techniques have been refined they follow some broad principles which are still valid today.

The case for inclusion assumes that the balance sheet purports to show the underlying financial strength of a business. The inclusion of brands is intended to help meet this objective and therefore provide a more realistic picture for shareholders.

Conveniently there are other benefits which flow from this approach. In the case of acquired brands it reduces the overall value attributable to goodwill although the ASB does not believe that this distinction can be made. However, given the uncertain nature of the goodwill debate if the arguments for recognizing brands at the time of acquisition are made powerfully enough then the distinction will be retained. This will become very important if the ASB moves to any kind of conclusion on goodwill.

Either by a reduction of goodwill for acquired brands or an increase in intangible assets from home-grown brands the effect is still to strengthen the balance sheet. That can be particularly beneficial, for instance, when calculating a company's gearing.

Where there is perhaps some divergence between acquired and home-grown brands is in the valuation process. If acquired brands are simply goodwill by another name, in other words the value attributed to intangible assets is merely a balancing number to reconcile the purchase price and net assets then the valuation exercise is rendered redundant. Only when there is some more scientific approach taken to valuing acquired brands does the process draw closer to the valuation of internally generated brands.

There are a number of possible methods for brand valuation. It could be the aggregate cost of all marketing advertising and research and development expenditure devoted to the brand over a specific period. This is effectively an extension of the cost capitalization principles employed in other areas of the balance sheet.

The valuation could also be established by applying a multiplier to the premium price that a branded product can achieve above the price of a non-branded product or by reference to consumer-related factors such as recognition or esteem. The market value could be used or a valuation could be derived by discounting the brand's future earnings potential.

Unfortunately there is no right or wrong way to go about valuing a brand. There are plus and minus points for all the above methods. The cost capitalization method does not, for example, make any allowance for the success of a brand. In fact it could give a misleading impression of the brand's value. If a company is being forced to spend heavily on advertising it may simply be because the brand is not that strong. The approach could be misleading both for the company and for investors. Using the brand premium as the starting point for valuation also has difficulties since it does not tell the whole story about a product's performance. The value of some brands has sometimes less to do with pricing and much more to do with its stature within a store.

This was illustrated many years ago when the soap powder manufacturers had a spat with Asda, the supermarket chain. At one store in the Midlands the manager insisted that he would only give orders to sales representatives who were prepared to come into the store on a Monday when it was closed to the public and stock up the shelves with their products. Proctor & Gamble refused to go along with this, arguing that their representatives were salesmen and not merchandisers. Asda therefore refused to stock P&G products. The dispute was settled, ironically by the intervention of Unilever, P&G's arch rival. Its representatives found that sales of its products were being hurt by the absence from the shelves of key P&G brands. Customers were coming to the store seeking Fairy Liquid or Daz and such was their brand loyalty that when they could not find these items they went elsewhere to do their shopping. It was the plea from Unilever to restock P&G products which solved the dispute. That is an incident which happened twenty years ago but it demonstrates that there is a power to a brand which goes beyond just price.

There is also a problem when there is no obvious generic competitor to a product which would render the premium method inappropriate.

A valuation technique based on consumer awareness would also have limitations. Although it might give some indication of what consumers thought about a product this is not always guaranteed to translate into some kind of commercial reality. A well-recognized brand that could not make any profit quite obviously has its limitations.

There are also limitations in using the market value approach. The price that someone is prepared to pay for a brand is clearly relevant. But given that brands are not traded on a regular basis it is hard to see where the benchmarks would come from to give a valuation any credibility.

The discounted earnings approach appears to have some merit but again this is fraught with difficulty. The further out the forecasts go the more difficult it is to predict with any certainty what the outturn will be.

These difficulties were recognized by RHM and its advisers Interbrand and the methodology they employed was therefore more sophisticated. The problem which arises, however, is that no matter what levels of sophistication are reached and no matter how boldly and confidently the underlying principles are stated, in the final analysis the process will rely on a high degree of subjectivity. Perhaps more worrying, however, is that the valuation is a much better guide to the past than it is a forecaster of the future. As we shall see later on the fact that an eloquent argument for valuation can be presented does not in the end do a great deal to meet the stated objective of providing a balance sheet which shows the underlying financial strength of the business.

Despite its limitations the RHM approach is still worthy of analysis since it covers the range of issues which need to be considered by any company which wants to take more account, in whatever form, of the value of its brands.

The RHM approach was designed to consider the marketing, financial and legal aspects of brands. It followed fundamental accounting concepts and Companies Acts requirements. It also allowed for regular revaluation and was suitable for both home-grown and acquired brands. The methodology has its foundation in the existing use of the brands and does not therefore concern itself with break-up or market values.

The most important factor, according to RHM, in determining a brand's value is its profitability particularly over a period of time. However, the approach goes beyond applying a multiplier to post-tax profits. The reasons for this are simple. Not all of a brand's profitability can be attributed to its name. It may have the attributes of a commodity product or may enjoy profitability because of the efficiencies of the distribution system. The elements not resulting directly from a brand's identity were therefore excluded. RHM also recognized that it was imprudent just to use one year's, potentially unrepresentative, profits and therefore its approach used a three-year weighted average post-tax profit figure as the starting point for the valuation exercise.

More intriguing, though, is the determination of the multiplier which must be applied to the post-tax profits. This was derived from an in-depth assessment of brand strength which required a detailed review of each brand, its positioning, the market in which it operated, competition, past performance, future plans and the risks the brand was exposed to. The brand strength was defined by RHM as a composite of seven weighted factors which were then scored according to clearly established and consistent guidelines. Those factors were:

- leadership (a brand which leads its market or sector is a more stable and valuable property than a brand lower down the order);
- stability (long-established brands which command consumer loyalty and have become part of the fabric of their markets are particularly valuable);
- market (brands in markets such as food and drink are intrinsically more valuable than brands in, for example, high technology or clothing since these are more vulnerable to changes in technology or fashion);
- internationality (brands which are global are inherently more valuable than those which are national or regional brands);

- trend (the overall long-term trend of the brand is an important measure of its ability to remain contemporary and relevant to consumer and hence of its value);
- support (those brand names which have received consistent investment and focused support must be regarded as more valuable than those which have not. While the amount spent in support of a brand is important the quality of that support is equally significant);
- protection (the strength and breadth of the brand's protection, such as through trademarks, is critical in assessing its value).

The brand strength is then used to derive the multiplier which will be applied to the brand's earnings. This works on the assumption that a brand with no strength is not a true brand. However, the more established the brand becomes then the more its value will increase although in the early years that increase will be quite gradual. Once the brand moves into number 2 in its market or when it secures the number 1 position the increase in the value then accelerates sharply. Once a brand becomes powerful internationally then the growth in value will increase but once more it will be at a slower rate.

The arguments provided by RHM were soundly based although the valuation element was easier to cope with than the capitalization element whereby these values were then included in the company's balance sheet. There is little doubt that brand valuation can be a useful management tool not least because it begins to focus attention on the workings of the brand. It allows management to see how each brand is performing and offers a comparative measure which could be useful for planning marketing strategies and assisting in investment prioritization.

However, a useful management tool is not necessarily such a useful tool for investors. For while RHM was gleefully boosting the balance sheet by including a brand valuation this unfortunately marked the beginning of a decline in its fortunes. In 1988, the year brand values were first included, the company made pre-tax profits of £156.6 million. By 1992, the year in which it lost its independence, the company was reporting pre-tax profits of just £92.6 million.

The analysis below shows the performance of the three dvisions which contain the bulk of RHM's brands over the same period.

	1988	1989	1990	1991	1992
	(£m)	(£m)	(£m)	(£m)	(£m)
Manor bakeries	26.9	23.4	17.8	18.5	10.9
Grocery products	32.5	30.2	28.8	35.4	39.9
Milling & bread baking	58.7	69.3	62.0	59.8	20.3

This analysis makes no allowances for brands which were sold during the period and it does not reflect any internal changes in the make-up of the individual divisions. However, it does put the theory of brand valuation in a real world context. Bearing in mind that profitability of the brands is regarded as a key element in determining value this analysis reveals the limitations of the exercise. For while the brands in their own right may remain strong when other factors are taken into consideration the profile of the group as a whole looks weaker. For investors it is the entirety of the picture which is most important.

Against the backdrop of the profits profile it is also useful to examine how the brand valuation process developed. Ignoring disposals and additions, in 1989 there was an upward revaluation of £20 million, in 1990 a downward revaluation of £7.3 million, in 1991 an upward revaluation of £20 million. In 1992 the analysis of valuations is unavailable but the total figures for brands had been reduced from £608 million in 1991 to £459 million in 1992.

By the time investors were alerted to this decline the company had all but lost its independence. It therefore begs the question of just how relevant the exercise had been in terms of providing investors with a better insight into the value of the company. Certainly it had no real effect in terms of the share price. Don't forget that before brands were put in the balance sheet Goodman Fielder Wattie had valued the company as being worth 465p a share which equates to a total value of £1.7 billion. Shortly after that the company put £678 million of brands on the balance sheet. When the company fell to Tomkins, in a bid which was supported by the board, the value of this 1992 offer was worth 260p a share in cash or £925 million for the whole company. The value of brands at this time was £459 million. In that period then the value of the company, as judged by a potential purchaser, had fallen by £775 million but the value of brands was judged to have fallen by just £219 million with the bulk of the decline coming in the last twelve months. It should be noted that in the stock market before the final bout of bid speculation which ultimately ended in the Tomkins take-over the shares were trading at 140p, some 70 per cent below the value of the Goodman Fielder Wattie offer four years earlier.

The basic problem with brand valuation in RHM's case is that its methodology was designed to look at the brands in isolation. But that is of no use to investors who must see the company in its entirety. There are often other intangible factors at work which could have implications for the valuation process. Just because those factors, such as management strategy, are not directly related to an individual brand is no reason to exclude it from the valuation, particularly if the implications are negative.

The debate on brands/goodwill will continue. And it is not just brands which will dominate the discussion. Reed Elsevier, the Anglo-Dutch publishing group, had £2,386 million of intangible assets in its 1993 balance sheet. The group's policy is described in the following terms: 'Publishing rights and titles, databases, exhibition rights and other intangible assets are stated at fair value on acquisition and are not subsequently revalued.'

Reed does not value internally generated intangibles but some newspaper groups do attribute a value to their home-grown titles.

Other items which crop up as intangibles in the balance sheet include development expenditure, software, licence agreements, programme rights, catalogue costs, patents, trademarks and even subscriber contracts.

Some are based on specific expenditure or acquisitions, others are more subjective. What they all have in common is that they are exploiting rules which are not designed to cope with their existence.

The consequences for the users of accounts are not always fully appreciated. Considerable benefits accrue from including intangible assets on the balance sheet. As we have seen the amounts can make a big difference to the impression given of a company's financial strength. A stronger reported asset base can also be important in terms of improving the overall gearing ratio which is a key indicator used to assess the relationship between borrowings and assets. Gearing ratios can often be used in banking covenants to impose some limits on the level of borrowings which can be made. If the asset base is artificially inflated then the ratio is much less relevant since it is no longer reflecting the true picture.

The problem remains, however, with finding a solution. The goodwill/intangibles debate will continue. But with some quite significant vested interests at stake the debate is not always guaranteed to be carried out in the most objective of climates. It will be an area of controversy for some time to come. It will also therefore be an area of creativity. With no immediate support from the ASB on hand the investors will simply have to remain vigilant. At least if users are aware of the consequences and implications of this complex issue they will be in a position to pose the questions in their own minds about what this really means for the company's broader financial position.

13. Deferred Taxation

Many investors sometimes give the appearance of sitting around with a sign on their eyes saying 'Please pull wool over'. The same cannot be said of the Inland Revenue which tends to have an altogether more vigilant outlook to the financial information presented to it. It may come as something of a surprise then to discover that taxation offers a quite fruitful opportunity for creative accounting. This is not because the Revenue is losing its touch. Far from it. It is both difficult and dangerous to attempt to manipulate the actual tax bill artificially. The flexibility arises from the mismatch between the Revenue's attitude to a companies tax liability and that adopted by the accounting standard setters.

At the heart of the mismatch are the differences between the tax treatment of some items of income and expenditure and their accounting treatment. These differences may be permanent because, for instance, some items of expenditure are disallowed for tax purposes or perhaps because income is tax free. They may also be temporary and are a function of what are known as timing differences, so called because they reflect the fact that a tax liability will arise at some later point in time.

It is these timing differences which give rise to deferred taxation. And it is the treatment of deferred taxation which presents the greatest creative accounting opportunities. It is no surprise then that the Accounting Standards Board is reviewing the rules dealing with deferred taxation and is threatening to impose a much tighter regime than the one which currently exists. Its discussion paper published in March 1995 gave the clearest indication yet that it intends to move to a system which will reduce flexibility and improve clarity.

The most common timing differences relate to capital expenditure. The depreciation which a company charges against fixed assets is disallowed for tax purposes. However, the Revenue does grant capital allowances which on plant and machinery are set at 25 per cent on a reducing balance basis. That means that the actual amount of the capital allowance which can be used to reduce taxable profits will fall over time. The depreciation charge, however, is likely to remain constant. In the early years of the asset's life the capital allowance will therefore exceed the depreciation charge so no actual tax liability occurs. In later years, however, the reducing balance basis on which capital allowances are calculated means that the allowance will be less than the depreciation charge. This reversal of the timing difference crystallizes the tax liability.

The shifting balance between capital allowances and depreciation is illustrated by the following simple example. Assume an asset cost £1,000 and is depreciated over ten years at an annual cost of £100:

	Year								
	1	*2*	*3*	*4*	*5*	*6*	*7*	*8*	*9*
Depreciation (£)	100	100	100	100	100	100	100	100	100
Capital allowance (£)	250	187.5	140.6	105.5	79.1	59.3	44.5	33.4	25
Surplus/(deficit) (£)	150	87.5	40.6	5.5	(20.9)	(40.7)	(55.5)	(66.6)	(75)

The surplus or deficit of allowances over depreciation will have a bearing on the actual tax paid for the year. It also accounts for the discrepancy between the theoretical tax rate on reported profits and what is paid. Assume the company has reported pre-tax profits of £1,000. That implies a tax charge of £330 on the basis of the 33 per cent rate being applied. However, in year one the taxable profit will not be £1,000 but £850 to reflect the surplus of capital allowances over depreciation. (£1,000 – £150 = £850). The tax at 33 per cent would then be only £280. When this is set against reported pre-tax profits of £1,000 the effective rate of tax falls to 28 per cent.

However, as the timing differences begin to reverse then the effective rate of tax begins to increase. In year 9 for instance still assuming reported pre-tax profits of £1,000, the taxable profits will be £1,075 (£1,000 + £75 – £1,075) since the depreciation charge is now well in excess of capital allowances. The tax payable would therefore be £355 suggesting an effective tax rate of 35.5 per cent on reported pre-tax profits of £1,000.

In order to smooth out these timing differences the accountancy profession devised rules dealing with the treatment of this deferred taxation. However, the standard setting process got off to a terrible start when it began in 1975. The original proposal was for companies to make provision for all material timing differences. This was both prudent and conservative. However, it immediately ran into stiff opposition and the profession was forced to tone the proposals down.

The most powerful argument levied against this full provision is still used today. This in essence demands that deferred taxation be seen in the context of a company's capital spending programme as a whole rather than by reference to individual assets. As has been shown, the timing differences for all assets are bound to reverse once the depreciation charge exceeds capital allowances. A liability is therefore bound to crystallize. However, it is argued that while the timing differences on a single asset may reverse when the differences are taken as a whole and in the context of an increasing capital expenditure programme, then capital allowances available in any year will always outweigh depreciation, thus rendering full provision unnecessary.

It was the power of this argument which ultimately paved the way, after a number of refinements, for the rules on deferred taxation as laid down by Statement of Standard Accounting Practice 15. Under SSAP15 companies are obliged to account for deferred tax on the liability method but with partial provision. In other words the full amount of the taxation liability is calculated but only a portion has to be provided for in the accounts. That provision will be based on the company's projections of the extent to which deferred tax liabilities will crystallize when its spending plans as a whole are considered.

The extent to which a company decides that a liability will not crystallize, thus making the timing difference permanent, can have a significant impact on the reported results for any period. The lower the partial provision the lower the reported tax charge. The lower the tax charge the higher the earnings per share. The lower the overall provision for deferred tax the higher a company's shareholder funds, therefore the lower its gearing.

The financial impact is significant and it is not surprising that there is something of an incentive for a company to demonstrate that its deferred tax liabilities are unlikely to crystallize. This can only be done on the basis of forecasts, judgements, assumptions, opinions and projections. Once you enter this territory then any pretence of objectivity must be abandoned. While SSAP15 does require the process to be carried out with appropriate care, attention and prudence the exercise is bound to be highly subjective.

The worry that the ASB has is that there is perhaps too much subjectivity. That means investors are not always getting access to the right information at the right time. Companies which take too robust a view of the strength of their capital expenditure programme expose themselves and their investors to an unfortunate double problem. One of the main reasons why deferred tax liabilities crystallize is because of a slow-down in the capital spending programme. Such a slow-down is often the management's response to a period of difficult trading. When cash flow is under pressure the easiest thing to cut is capital expenditure. However, a reduction in capital spending can result in deferred tax payments falling due. The upshot is increased pressure on the cash flow at a time when the company can least afford it.

However, there are intellectual arguments which can also be levied against the partial provision approach to deferred tax. To start with it tends to disregard the basic principle of prudence whereby liabilities are accounted for as soon as they are recognized. With partial provision, even though a timing difference is bound to reverse, the liability is not always recognized. Secondly the SSAP15 approach relies upon a group of transactions being treated collectively rather than in isolation with each being treated on its own merits.

Against this backdrop the ASB has understandably taken an interest in the subject. It has given consideration to whether Britain should move to the full provision method which is favoured in the US for instance. Under the full provision approach a company would be obliged to account for all its deferred tax liabilities. All timing differences would be provided for even if they will be offset on reversal by future timing differences. The ASB is inclined to take the full provisioning route although it offers the prospect of some discounting of the increased liability which would mitigate the financial impact.

Any move to a straightforward full provisioning approach would have important financial consequences. In a thoughtful and far-sighted piece of research published in October 1994 City brokers Hoare Govett argued that the new method, if adopted by the ASB, would wipe 10 per cent off the stock market's earnings. Some individual companies would see their earnings per share slashed in excess of 40 per cent and many companies would see their gearing increase sharply as shareholders' funds were eroded.

The financial impact of a change would in some cases be very material. It is not surprising then that the ASB has encountered some resistance. Although it is the argument that the full provision method will be distortive since in cases of a rising capital expenditure programme the allowances will always offset depreciation which dominates, there is no mistaking the subtext. Those companies which can see their reported earnings per share being slashed are clearly unhappy with the prospect of a change.

To some extent the worries about overprovision for deferred taxation would be mitigated by any discounting of the potential liability to reflect the fact that the tax would not fall due for payment for several years. However, while this may help soften the blow for those companies worried about their earnings profile it also injects further complexities into the arena. The clarity and objectivity inherent in the full provisioning approach would therefore begin to be undermined. The danger would be that uncertainties about the assumptions put together about its expected capital spending and timing difference profile would merely be replaced by uncertainties about the assumptions underpinning an assessment of the time value of money.

On the grounds that the rules as laid down by SSAP15 are too flexible and allow companies to exercise just too much judgement when assessing deferred taxation provisions then the time is right for a change. Given the auditing profession's apparent reluctance to exercise too much of its own judgement in the more contentious accounting areas it falls to the ASB to set a standard which is altogether more prescriptive. That therefore favours introduction of the full provision approach.

A new standard would also provide an opportunity to revisit some of the other uncertainties which surround deferred taxation. The treatment of tax losses, particularly when those losses are anticipated rather than incurred, is in need of repair. There is also a need for greater clarity over the role of fixed asset revaluations in the deferred tax process. The treatment of overseas earnings can also create uncertainty. Finally there is a need to reassess the relationship between deferred taxation and Advance Corporation Tax.

All of the above make their own contribution to the collective complexity of the deferred taxation question. That complexity tends to discourage the outside investor from prying too closely into the issue. This lack of attention has made it in the past a quite intriguing theatre of operation. However, with the ASB preparing to take a more robust stance then the opportunities for further creativity will be much reduced.

14. Investment Criteria

The preceding chapters will have been a little depressing for those who thought that a set of accounts was supposed to form some kind of reliable basis on which to make a judgement about a company's performance. Sadly this is an attribute which cannot be taken for granted. In the majority of cases a financial report will indeed represent a true and fair view of the company's affairs. The big problem is that it is still very difficult to identify the all important exceptions where the accounts are masking an altogether more disturbing picture. The fact remains that despite the improvements in the rules, accounts preparation is still heavily reliant upon subjective judgements. The quality of the product will, therefore, depend largely on the quality of the judgements.

Unless there is a wholesale change in the way that accounts are constructed then the rules will remain necessarily flexible. That means judgement will continue to play an important part irrespective of what the Accounting Standards Board does. The ASB has gone a long way to closing some obvious loopholes and stamping out the more flagrant abuses. However, it is never going to reach a position, nor would it want to, where it can marshal judgements down the same precise lines. The ASB is developing a more constructive and clearer framework than the one it inherited. It remains, however, only a framework.

The question then for the user is how to make any sense of a set of accounts. Perhaps the most important defence against the accounting traps which have been set is to develop a healthy cynicism about the relevance and reliability of the financial reporting process. Too many people like to believe in the notion of the definable profit. That is sometimes a function of ignorance and sometimes a function of convenience. In the City, for instance, it is often easier to focus on the quantity of earnings rather than the quality. When prices have to be struck in an instant and deals have to be done on the spur of the moment it is not always appropriate to indulge in a lengthy assessment of the provisioning process. The convenient common denominator of the stated earnings is an appropriate measurement sometimes merely because it is not in dispute.

For those who do not need the convenience of the single definable number then there is no reason to sign up to the concept. Once a user makes the quantum leap to cynicism then the annual report will be seen in an entirely different light. This is not to say that you should simply sneer at the accounts and disregard them completely. Instead they should be viewed with the sceptical eye which will ensure that they can become a valuable source of questions rather than the sole source of answers.

Merely by taking a questioning approach based on the knowledge that the figures are representative, judgemental and subjective will transform the attitude which is taken towards the annual report. This rather imposing and sometimes intimidating document will begin to shrink in stature. Its foreboding presence conjured up by the unfriendly presentation and the complexities of accounting speak will become much less threatening once it is accepted that much of it is based on guesswork.

With this pyschological barrier cleared it then becomes possible to deal with the document on more equal terms. That still leaves the problem that many financial reports remain user hostile. Many sets of accounts give the impression that they can only be read by qualified accountants or City professionals. This is an irritation but it can be dealt with simply by applying a high degree of patience and concentration. The temptation to dismiss parts of the accounts as being unpenetrable waffle is understandable but it should be resisted. It is only by working your way very carefully through the accounts that any value can be extracted from them.

Once you have worked up the confidence to question the accounts the single most important element to focus on is cash. No matter how skilled the creative accountant is he cannot create cash where none exists. He can delay and defer, he can accelerate and allocate, but he cannot conjure up cash flow. Cash is only king because it is the lifeblood of the business. Without it bills cannot get paid and when bills do not get paid then a company is in trouble. A company can hide away provisions for redundancy payments in the balance sheet, it can disguise them in the profit and loss account. But if the money is not there to pay the workers as they leave the factory then the house of cards will come tumbling down.

The user does not get all the help which might be expected in his pursuit of cash flow. As we have seen there are a number of areas where specific departures from cash flow are required. However, there is compensation in the shape of Financial Reporting Standard 1 which deals with cash-flow statements. It may be pertinent that this was the first of the ASB's standards and perhaps reflect the importance which is attached to cash flow. There is little doubt that it is a big improvement on the old statement of sources and applications of funds although there are still question marks about whether it gives the user an insight into the company's own practical day-to-day thinking on cash flow.

One of the objectives of FRS1 is to assist users of financial statements in their assessment of the reporting entity's liquidity, viability and financial adaptability. It certainly goes some way to meeting this objective but the sense that the FRS1 document is one which will be regularly used as part of the internal management planning process is still lacking. Throughout the recession of the early nineties there was an increasing move by companies to focus much more closely on cash flow. When times got hard the corporate sector realized pretty quickly that cash is a scarce resource which is well worth conserving. The focus on cash flow is unlikely to become too blurred when the going gets a bit easier because that focus has reaped dividends for those who were prepared to pay cash the attention it deserves.

If companies regard cash flow as an essential feature of the decision-making process then investors should do likewise. The starting point will be the cash-flow statement as presented in the accounts but it will have to be supplemented by other observations and questions.

FRS1 requires a company to analyse cash flows under the following standard headings: operating activities, returns on investment and servicing of finance, taxation, investing activities and financing. Within these categories a company will give quite comprehensive information, supplemented by notes, which provide a useful guide to the overall cash-flow profile of the group. There are shortcomings but the ASB is seeking views on how the standard is working in practice and the prospects for further improvement are therefore good.

By focusing on cash rather than profits it is possible to secure a feel for where the pressure points for a business are developing. If a company is relying too much on the disposal of fixed assets to generate cash then it poses questions. Similarly if there is a mismatch between increasing borrowings and reducing investment then there may also be problems. The aim here is to assess the strength of the operating cash flow which the company generates.

In essence the user has to become something of a detective. He must imagine what the economic and commercial reality of a situation will be and see how this matches with figures as presented. Wherever there are signs of a mismatch then there is cause for further investigation. In this context it is particularly valuable to look at key payments which the company has to make such as dividends and taxation.

The dividend is a highly significant indicator of the company's welfare. More importantly it involves a cash payment. A company which is showing apparently high reported profits or very strong cash flow yet which is holding or cutting its dividend is either being excessively prudent or something is not quite right. Similarly a company which has a low tax payment relative to reported profits will also merit closer scrutiny. The Inland Revenue tends to be a more rigorous taskmaster than the investor. It is not overly enamoured with those who seek to evade and indeed avoid taxation. The actual payment will give some feel for the underlying profitability. It is not necessarily a sign of imprudence. The efficient corporate tax manager can bring considerable benefits for investors. Similarly international groups with activities in low tax areas will clearly secure the advantage of a lower tax charge. However, as a specific cash payment to an independent third party the actual tax bill will provide a useful yardstick.

The cash flow statement will give some indication of the impact of provisions on the overall profile. As we have seen these provisions can be a very effective way of protecting the profit and loss account. They are the source, though, of a great mismatch between profits and cash flow. They are therefore worthy of particular attention. One shorthand means of getting a feel for how extensively provisioning has been used is to examine a company's accounts over a period of time. Add up the retained profits over perhaps a four-year period. Theoretically revenue reserves should have been boosted by the same amount. If a company has been taking provisions direct to the balance sheet this will be reflected in the shortfall between the increase in revenue reserves as disclosed in the balance sheet over the period under review and the total ascertained by adding together retained profits as shown in the four profit and loss accounts.

A close analysis of reserves will shed light on the underlying strength of the business. If, for instance, investors had focused on balance-sheet reserves rather than the profit and loss account it might have given some warning of the foreign currency problems which were stacking up at Polly Peck.

One way that companies can avoid depleting reserves is to boost their assets and as the chapter on goodwill shows this can be a particular problem when dealing with intangibles. There may well be legitimate arguments for keeping those intangibles intact but any mismatch between the operating profits generated by these assets and the value attributed to the intangible assets themselves will need to be examined more closely.

Tangible assets too must be seen in the context of economic reality. At a time of falling property prices it becomes harder for companies to justify not making any adjustment to the valuation.

It is also important to scrutinize quite carefully the accounting policies set out by the company. These are often couched in quite cumbersome terms which do not make for easy reading. The converse of this is a blandness which gives virtually nothing away. However, it is worth persevering with. Although it may be difficult to gauge the appropriateness of the judgements which are ultimately made the policies do provide a starting point and will give some limited feel for areas of contention. Of particular note will be those policies which have been changed. Sometimes there will be a very good reason for the alteration perhaps to comply with a new ASB ruling. Where the company is making the change arbitrarily there will be a need to probe a little more closely. Often the financial implications of the change will be provided which may give some insight into the motivation for the switch.

Special focus on these specific areas, with the mismatch always in mind, taken with a close examination of all the notes to the accounts, which will normally give much more detail and information than the primary statement, will allow the user to build up some kind of picture of the business and identify the areas of uncertainty.

There will then be the opportunity to see how this analysis squares with the more accessible review of the business which will be found in the glossy part of the accounts. The chairman's statements, the chief executive's review and the analysis of operations are now common parts of the accounts. However, their value has in the past been somewhat limited.

Too often a potentially valuable commentary on the company and its prospects has been reduced to little more than public relations hype. The front half of the accounts can sometimes appear like a promotional pamphlet rather than a considered and thoughtful supplement to the annual accounts. These reviews rely too much on the past and give very little guidance to the future.

Recognizing this missed opportunity the ASB has produced a statement setting out what it expects companies to produce by way of an Operating and Financial Review. The statement has no mandatory application and unfortunately is little more than a precis of what it regards as best practice. Although it has received the endorsement of leading finance directors compliance with its principles remains voluntary. That is a pity since the OFR has the potential to be one of the most useful elements of any set of accounts. It is true that the better companies are already going a long way towards and sometimes beyond the ASB model. However, these progressive companies tend to be the ones where investors have least to fear. It is those businesses which choose a less constructive approach to their OFR where there is more to fear.

It will not always be obvious where a company has complied with the ASB's recommendations. To assist the user in assessing how far the company has gone in complying with the broad principles the ASB's model code provides useful guidelines. This can act as an investor check-list which can be used to assist in establishing the relevance of the corporate prose to a fuller understanding of the company's financial position.

The essential features are as follows:

- It should be written in a clear and concise style which is readily understood and should include only matters that are likely to be significant to investors.
- It should be balanced and objective dealing even-handedly with both good and bad aspects of the business.
- It should refer back to comments made in previous statements where these have not been borne out by events.

- It should contain analytical discussion rather than merely numerical analysis.
- It should follow a top-down structure discussing individual aspects of the business in the context of a discussion of the business as a whole.
- It should explain the reasons for and effect of any change in accounting policies.
- It should make clear how any ratios or other numerical information given relate to the financial statements.
- It should include a discussion of trends and factors underlying the business that have affected the results but are not expected to continue in the future, and of known events, trends and uncertainties that are expected to have an impact on the business in the future.

These are the broad criteria which should be used to assess the overall structure of the front of book comments from the company's senior executives. Beyond this there are some specific areas which the user will want to see addressed.

The basic operating review, as distinct from the financial review, should allow the reader to understand the dynamics of the various businesses. It should identify the main influences on the results and explain how they interrelate and explain the main factors underpinning the business. In particular it should highlight those factors which have varied in the past or are expected to change in the future.

There should be a comprehensive analysis of the operating results right down to the pre-tax level which focuses on the segments and divisions which are relevant to an understanding of the performance as a whole. It should examine changes in the industry or environment in which the company operates and indicate how these have affected the results. The kinds of thing to look for are changes in market conditions, new products and services introduced or announced, changes in market share or position, changes in turnover and margins, changes in exchange and inflation rates, details of acquisitions and disposals and of new investments or closures. When acquisitions have been material you would expect to see some discussion of whether it has lived up to expectations.

When looking at the dynamics of the business the user should be able to establish which are the main factors and influences which have an effect on the business. These may not necessarily have had an impact in the year under review but will remain important to the business. In essence it should be possible to identify the risks and uncertainties which a company faces, how it sets about managing them and what the potential impact could be. Matters which could be relevant include: scarcity of raw materials, skill shortages, patents, licences and franchises, dependence on major suppliers or customers, product liability, health and safety, environmental protection costs and liabilities, self-insurance, exchange rate fluctuations, inflation rates.

It should be possible for a user presented with this kind of information to establish a reasonable risk sensitivity profile of the group. This changes the nature of the financial review from being a passive historical document to being a more pro-active forward-looking work.

In keeping with this theme it is also important to identify the action the management has taken both to secure and enhance profitability in the future. The user will therefore want to see evidence of the discretionary action and expenditure undertaken with this purpose in mind. Clearly capital expenditure is important here. The amounts can be significant and capital projects will often have long lead times. Therefore the reader will want to see discussion of both past and planned expenditure identifying the business segments and geographical areas which will be targeted for capital spending. Some analysis of the benefits should be given.

Although capital spending is important there are other areas of expenditure which can have a significant influence on protecting and improving profitability. The users should be conscious that absolute levels of expenditure in these areas are probably less relevant than the impact of changes to the spending programme. Areas to be conscious of include:

marketing and advertising, training, refurbishment and maintenance, research, development, technical support programmes.

This type of information should help give some impression of what measures have been taken to protect profitability. It is also useful to identify the actual performance during the year under review in terms of how it relates to the shareholders' own well-being. This means that the company executives should be presenting some discussion of the overall return attributable to shareholders by way of dividends and increases in shareholders' funds. This should involve some reference to the recognized gains and losses statement which must now be provided. There should also be an explanation of the relationship between profits, earnings and dividends.

The very best operating reviews will include some discussion of accounting policies and in particular the assumptions and judgements which underpin them. Ideally they will give some insight into the most important judgements which can make such a big difference to the figures which are reported.

Moving now to the financial review the principal aim here should be to explain to the user the capital structure of the business, its treasury position and the dynamics of its financial position.

Users will therefore be looking for a discussion of the capital structure of the business in terms of the maturity profile of debt and capital instruments used together with analysis of the currency and interest rate structure. In particular it should be possible to assess the capital funding and treasury policies and objectives. This should cover risk management and also details of implementation. Treasury management has become an increasingly important part of a company's operations and so it merits closer attention. Users should therefore be looking for details of the manner in which treasury activities are controlled, the currencies in which borrowings are made and in which cash is held, the extent to which borrowings are at fixed interest rates, the use of financial instruments for hedging purposes and the extent to which foreign currency investments are hedged by currency and other instruments.

On taxation the user will be looking for some explanation of any mismatch between the standard tax rate and the actual rate together with some analysis of the main components of the tax charge.

As we have already seen in this chapter cash is a critical indicator of how a company is performing. A good financial review will provide further discussion of cash flow and of the company's overall liquidity position. Some reference should be made to the funding requirements of the group. There should also be a discussion on any restrictions on the ability to transfer funds within the group such as exchange controls. Any covenants with lenders should also be outlined setting out the implications for credit facilities. If covenants are being renegotiated, or where they have been breached or are likely to be breached, then again some explanation should be provided.

In the real world this role model operating and financial review is unlikely to be seen in its entirety. However, if the user comes to this glossy portion of accounts armed with some idea of the perfect world solution then it represents a valuable basis on which to begin asking questions.

If the accounts as a whole are seen as the starting point for further investigation rather than as an end in themselves then the value of the document increases significantly. This is very much how the Accounting Standards Board sees the financial report and it does no harm whatsoever to mirror its attitude. The ASB is, after all, charged with the responsibility of improving the quality of financial reporting. The rules it is constructing are based on this basic philosophy of provoking questions.

By the same token it is important to look at the accounts with a number of key indicators in mind. The ASB has been trying to persuade investors, particularly those in the City, to get away from the notion that a single headline performance indicator is required. The ASB believes that it is far more important to look at a range of figures and again its rules are being formulated with this in mind. The prudent user will accept the ASB's advice and look at a range of indicators.

By taking this widespread and questioning approach with a particular focus on cash and with an alert eye for any mismatches it will allow the accounts to take their place as a relevant and important document in the investment analysis process. They can never be used in isolation and it remains important for users who have an interest in a particular company to spread their information database as widely as possible. An understanding of the real world in which a company operates provides a context in which the accounts themselves can be judged.

It is too easy to dismiss accounts as an irrelevancy since at the end of the day they represent the most comprehensive statement of a company's financial performance. It is argued that the quality of a company's management is a better guide to its prospects than the annual report. There is no doubt that good management is critical. However, the report is the tangible manifestation of an intangible quality. It should not be ignored.

15. In Conclusion

Creative accounting is still very much with us. The Accounting Standards Board has gone a long way in removing some of the most odious abuses but by definition it cannot remove entirely the flexibility from accounts preparation. The potential for either a gentle massage or a vigorous rub-down therefore remains.

Ironically the question of whether the situation improves lies not with the standards setters but with those who are very much at the heart of the financial reporting process. It is in the gift of accounts preparers, auditors and users to decide what kind of reporting environment this country is blessed with.

The ASB stands on the threshold of a new phase of its short career. It is a phase which will be crucial in determining the long-term shape of the financial reporting regime in the UK. The challenge the ASB faces is to persuade all those who are involved with the financial reporting process that excellence is a goal worth pursuing.

That cannot be taken for granted. For while many are prepared to pay lip service to the objective, the words are easier than the action.

Already the ASB has run smack into some quite vehement opposition from the accounts preparers with its new rules on acquisition accounting. FRS7 dealing with Fair Values in Acquisition Accounting met with a robust response from the 100 Group of Finance Directors. It said: 'Abuses should be dealt with by tightening of the wording and definitions in Accounting Standards, and through proper policing by the

external auditors, not by distorting basic accounting concepts
. . . The 100 Group's view is that it does no service to users of
accounts by introducing such distortions to the profit and loss
account.'

This is fighting talk. It is based on genuine disquiet with the
ASB's approach. It therefore sends out a worrying message and
puts the preparers in direct confrontation with the standard
setters.

It must be hoped that this outburst was just a last
opportunity for the 100 Group to air its deeply felt grievances.
Having got things off its chest perhaps there will be a return to
the more constructive relationship which had up until that
point typified the ASB's dealing with industry.

The problem is, however, that from now on the issues with
which the ASB has to grapple will become much more
contentious and complex. At some point it must, for instance,
grasp the nettle represented by the treatment of brands and
goodwill. It is hard to see how a solution can be devised which
will be both effective and acceptable to all parties. The worry,
therefore, is that accounts preparers will become disenchanted
with the standard setting process. If they lose confidence in the
ASB then its job will become very difficult. It is useful to recall
that when the accountancy procession was grappling with the
question of inflation accounting it was the accounts preparers
who were quite influential in the ultimate withdrawal of an
accounting standard.

FRS7 is not the only publication to have attracted a degree of
hostility. The exposure draft dealing with Related Party
Disclosures has also attracted a degree of criticism. That is to
be expected insofar as the draft is an integral part of the
consultation process and interested parties are bound to put
their views in quite forthright terms. The thinking behind the
draft is to force companies into greater disclosure about the
nature of the relationships they have with other companies
which they either control or influence. It would also demand
greater disclosure of deals between directors and their
immediate families.

The whole question of related party transactions is fraught with problems. The exposure draft is very much in the anti-fraud mould. While disclosure of itself is no guarantee against wrongdoing there is no doubt that it can provide an amber light to alert investors to the fact that there are potential areas of conflict worthy of further exploration.

Immediately, however, the exposure received a hostile reception. Criticisms ranged from the burden of excessive disclosure required to concerns that important information would be given away to competitors. The Confederation of British Industry was worried that the costs of implementing any standard would outweigh the benefits which would accrue from it.

These are no doubt heart-felt criticisms. Yet they are targeted at a standard which is specifically designed to alert users to the potential for fraud. This poses a number of intriguing questions which will have to be answered over the coming months. First, is the ASB now entering territory where there is bound to be a conflict between the interests of preparers and those of accounts users? It is interesting for instance that users were much happier with the tough line the ASB took on fair value provisions in acquisition accounting than preparers. With the related parties exposure draft there were few criticisms from users of proposals which were after all very much for their benefit.

If that line of divergence of interest has been crossed then it poses some big difficulties for the ASB. So far there has been a communality of interest between preparers and users. If the quality of financial reporting can be improved then the level of understanding is also increased. That works to the advantage of company and shareholder alike. We are now seeing, however, the first hints of a split in that alliance.

That gives rise to the second question. If preparers are going to find themselves in open confrontation with the ASB where will the accounts users pledge their allegiance? This is a crucial question. If the ASB can get the wholehearted support of the accounts users and in particular the institutional investment community then its prospects of securing a quality financial reporting framework are greatly enhanced.

The backing of the big investors is essential for the ASB. It is they who have some genuine influence over the companies they own. They can exert genuine pressure by supporting those companies with good financial reporting and neglecting those whose accounting is less rigorous.

In theory it is the big investors who have most to gain from the ASB's endeavours. They have the technical expertise to cope with the inbuilt complexities of accounts preparation so are ideally placed to secure the greater understanding which stems from the ASB's work. Institutional investor frustration and disappointment with reckless accounting of the eighties was after all instrumental in the creation of the ASB.

There is just a sense, however, that the City's investment community is not so wedded to the notion of improved financial reporting as it sometimes thinks. Everyone agrees that they want better accounts but there are fewer who can come forward with constructive ideas on what this really means and how it might be usefully achieved.

What is also unclear is how investors will respond once economic recovery is well and truly underway. The ASB's work so far has been conducted against a backdrop of recession and retrenchment. The frenzied corporate activity which typified the late eighties has faded away in the more austere times of the early nineties. In some cases survival has been more important than growth. However, once the economic climate becomes less hostile and when growth is firmly back on the investors' agenda it is unclear just how meticulous shareholders will be in perusing the accounting policies which underpin the reported financial performance. The quest for earnings growth can breed some very bad accounting habits.

For the time being that is not an issue. As the bid for Lasmo in 1994 from its rival Enterprise Oil demonstrated there is still a general fascination with the question of creative accounting. As part of its defence Lasmo raised some questions about the accounting used by Enterprise. It created a flurry of interest even though the matters referred to had long been overtaken by events. Perhaps more importantly it demonstrated just how difficult it is to agree on a wrong or a right way of preparing accounts. When the Take-over Panel was asked to adjudicate on the accounting spat it was unable to come up with a definitive ruling. And why should it? Accounting is dominated by matters of opinion and judgement.

That was a useful reminder to investors of the creative accounting issue. More importantly it once again highlighted the importance of auditors in the process. It is they who carry a high degree of influence in assessing whether an accounting policy is appropriate or not.

The problem here is that there is an increasing tendency for the auditing profession to fall back on the ASB in seeking clearer guidance on how the rules should be interpreted. Although the ASB would be happy dealing with broad principles there is increasing pressure from the auditing profession for more prescriptive standards. There seems to be a fear of exercising judgement.

The worry is that matters of interpretation will be constantly thrown back to the standard setters, probably in the shape of the Urgent Issues Task Force, for clarification. The first hint of what lies in store is to be found in the standards on off-balance-sheet financing and complex capital instruments. Here the reader finds a relatively short basic standard followed by pages of illustrative examples.

It is a basic rule of nature that an illustrative example never fits any real-life transaction precisely. You are therefore left with a transaction which has only attributes of an illustration. The simplest way of dealing with the uncertainty created over what is the appropriate accounting treatment would be, effectively, to refer the whole transaction back to the UITF by letting it decide whether there had been compliance with the relevant accounting standard.

This would be most unhelpful. The result would be a move away from broad principles to prescriptive regulation which is not only undesirable but would also be secured by a series of random ad hoc rulings. That could only undermine the entire standard setting process.

The auditing profession therefore needs to regain some of its self confidence and begin again to exercise the firm judgement which in the final analysis can only enhance its reputation. That is easier said than done and the pressures imposed upon the profession make the job increasingly difficult. However, a strong and clearly independent auditing profession is a prerequisite of any standard setting system which relies heavily on judgement.

There is no doubt that if the auditor could revisit its relationship with the shareholders, who it has to be remembered they actually report to, then the prospects for a sustainable improvement in the financial reporting process would be greatly increased.

This can only happen, however, if there is a genuine commitment from all parties involved to the basic principles on which the ASB is basing its work. That may involve some painful decisions. It may at times involve companies in unwelcome reductions in reported profitability. However, providing the investment community at large understands and supports the underlying issues that will not bring the penalty which is sometimes feared by accounts preparers. Accounting policies can do many things but they cannot generate the cash which is the lifeblood of any business. A tougher standard setting regime may change the numbers and the way in which they are presented but it cannot change the fundamentals of the business. If companies and their shareholders, supported by their auditors, remember this then no one has anything to fear from what, after all, should be nothing more than the pursuit of clearer understanding.

This country will ultimately end up with the quality of financial reporting and the standard setting regime it deserves. What that will be is in the hands of shareholders, companies and the auditing profession. The ASB is a mere catalyst for change. It can offer up the opportunities for improvement but only those with most to gain, or lose, can seize them and exploit them.

However, if those opportunities are spurned then they will be gone and lost for ever. If we are to be condemned to a financial reporting system based on mediocrity, compromise and confusion then we will have only ourselves to blame.